GUIDE TO LIFE-SPAN DEVELOPMENT FOR FUTURE NURSES

Terri T. Combs
Indiana University-Purdue University
at Indianapolis

Brown & Benchmark
PUBLISHERS

Madison, WI   Dubuque   Guilford, CT   Chicago   Toronto   London
Mexico City   Caracas   Buenos Aires   Madrid   Bogotá   Sydney

ISBN 0-697-35557-8

Printed in the United States of America by Times Mirror Higher Education Group, Inc., 2460 Kerper Boulevard, Dubuque, Iowa, 52001

10 9 8 7 6 5 4 3 2 1

CONTENTS

SECTION I INTRODUCTION

The purpose of this text is to help future nurses learn or review the life-span development concepts most likely to be tested on licensure exams for nurses. This is done by (1) reviewing the developmental concepts most often included on the National Council Licensure Examination for Registered Nurses (NCLEX-RN) and on the National Council Licensure Examination for Practical Nurses (NCLEX-PN), (2) providing review questions to test knowledge of the concepts presented in this guide, and (3) including questions from Mosby's Review Questions for NCLEX-RN (1995) and from Mosby's Comprehensive Review of Nursing (1996) to give students practice with test items similar to those on the actual nursing licensure exams.

This guide divides the review content into four sections: (1) Introduction to Development, Prenatal Development and Birth, (2) Infancy and Toddlerhood, (3) Childhood and Adolescence, and (3) Adulthood and Death. Each section begins with a review of concepts and ends with a case study and 30 multiple-choice questions to assess knowledge of material presented in that section. These sections will help readers acquire, review, and test knowledge of life span development.

Following the concept reviews and questions, two practice tests will give students experience in applying developmental concepts in a nursing context. Each practice test consists of 50 multiple-choice items drawn from Mosby's general nursing exam review guides. They include questions that test knowledge of development across the entire lifespan and require integration of information across developmental and nursing domains. Rationale for the answers to the practice tests are given to help students understand why each choice would be correct or incorrect.

This guide is intended to be useful at two points during students' nursing educations. First, when students are enrolled in a life-span development course, and second, when students are reviewing for the nursing licensure exam. While students are taking a life span development course, the concept review will help them pinpoint the concepts most likely to be tested later on the licensure exam. This will enable them to focus on the more complete and comprehensive coverage of those concepts in their regular life-span textbook. Students who have had few or no nursing courses at this point will not yet have the knowledge needed to answer the practice test questions at the end of the guide. They should not expect to be able to answer them and, instead, should use practice tests to get a general idea of how the developmental concepts they are currently learning will later be integrated with nursing information on the licensure exam.

When students are nearing the end of their nursing education and are preparing to take the nursing licensure exam, this guide will once again be useful. Students can use it to refresh their knowledge of the developmental concepts most likely to be covered on the NCLEX exams and to practice answering questions similar to those on the actual exams. The questions on the practice tests were intended for use with the NCLEX-RN, but many of the same concepts are needed for the NCLEX-PN. Both NCLEX exams use computerized testing and can vary in length. The NCLEX-RN has a minimum of 75 questions and a maximum of 265 questions. The NCLEX-PN also has a minimum of 75 questions but has a maximum of about 205 questions. Both exams require the test-taker to integrate information about growth and development across clinical areas such as pediatrics, women's health and obstetrics, and medical-surgical nursing. Knowledge about physical, cognitive, and social functioning from prenatal development, infancy, childhood, adolescence, adulthood, and death is needed. On the NCLEX-RN, approximately 12-18% of the questions reflect the need for education and health promotion, the client need that is most likely to draw on knowledge of development. On the NCLEX-PN, about 15-21% of the questions concern health promotion/maintenance. By studying the reviews and completing the practice tests in this guide, students will gain valuable experience working with concepts often tested on the NCLEX exams.

SECTION II INTRODUCTION TO DEVELOPMENT, PRENATAL DEVELOPMENT, AND BIRTH CONCEPT REVIEW

Introduction to Life-Span Development Review

I. **Characteristics of the life-span perspective (Baltes, 1987)**
    A. Development is **lifelong**: Gains and losses in development occur throughout the life cycle
    B. Development is **multidimensional**: Development occurs in the biological, cognitive, and social domains
    C. Development is **multidirectional**: Some aspects of development may be increasing while others are declining or not changing
    D. Development is **plastic**: Development can be modified by life circumstances to some extent
    E. Development is **embedded in history**: Development is influenced by historical conditions
    F. Development is **multidisciplinary**: Development is studied by a number of disciplines, including psychology, sociology, anthropology, neuroscience, and medicine
    G. Development is **contextual**: Development occurs in the context of a person's biological makeup, physical environment, and social, historical, and cultural contexts
        1. **Normative age-graded influences:** Biological and environmental influences that are similar for individuals in a particular age group (e.g., puberty, beginning school)
        2. **Normative history-graded influences:** Biological and environmental influences that are associated with history; influences that are common to people of a particular generation (e.g., the Depression, the AIDS epidemic)
        3. **Nonnormative life events:** Unusual occurrences that have a major impact on an individual's life; the occurrence, pattern, and sequence of these events are not applicable to most individuals (e.g., death of a parent at a young age, getting a serious illness, winning a lottery)
II. **Processes of development**
    A. **Biological processes** involve changes in the individual's physical nature (e.g., height and weight gains, cardiovascular decline)
    B. **Cognitive processes** involve changes in the individual's thought, intelligence, and language (e.g. memory development, learning to speak in sentences)
    C. **Socioemotional processes** involve changes in the individual's relationships with other people, changes in emotions, and changes in personality (e.g., children's play, relationships with parents)
III. **Periods of development**
    A. **Prenatal development**
        1. From conception to birth
        2. Tremendous growth occurs
    B. **Infancy**
        1. From birth to 18 to 24 months of age
        2. Extreme dependence on adults
        3. Many psychological events just beginning (e.g., language, sensorimotor coordination)
    C. **Early childhood**
        1. From 18 to 24 months until 5 or 6 years
        2. Sometimes called the preschool years
        3. Learn to become more self-sufficient and to care for themselves
        4. Develop school readiness skill
        5. Play with peers a lot
        6. First grade marks the end of this period

D. **Middle and late childhood**
1. From 6 to 11 years of age
2. Sometimes called the elementary school years
3. Basic academic skills of reading, writing, and math are mastered
4. Exposed to the larger world and its culture
5. Achievement becomes more important
6. Self-control increases

E. **Adolescence**
1. From 10 to 12 years of age until 18 to 22 years of age
2. Begins with rapid physical changes of puberty
3. Striving towards independence
4. Achieving identity
5. More time spent outside family

F. **Early adulthood**
1. Begins in the late teens or early twenties and lasts through the thirties
2. Establishing personal and economic independence
3. Career development often important
4. May select a mate
5. May start a family, rear children

G. **Middle adulthood**
1. Begins at about 35 to 45 years of age and lasts until the sixties
2. Expanding personal and social involvement
3. Increased responsibility
4. Assisting the next generation
5. Reaching and maintaining satisfaction in one's career

H. **Late adulthood**
1. Begins in the sixties or seventies and lasts until death
2. Adjusting to decreasing strength and health
3. Adjustment to new social roles
4. Retirement
5. Life review

IV. **Developmental issues**
A. **Nature-nurture issue**
1. **Nature** refers to an organism's biological inheritance
2. **Nurture** refers to environmental experiences
3. "Nature" proponents claim biological inheritance is the most important influence on development
4. "Nurture" proponents claim that environmental experiences are the most important influence
5. Most developmentalists currently view the **interaction** of nature and nurture rather than either factor alone to be most important

B. **Continuity-discontinuity issue**
1. Developmentalists who emphasize **continuity** view development as involving gradual, cumulative change from conception to death
2. Developmentalists who emphasize **discontinuity** view development as occurring in distinct stages over the life span.
3. Both views may be correct with some aspects of development being continuous while others are discontinuous

C. **Stability-change issue**
1. Developmentalists with a **stability** perspective contend that as we age, we become older renditions of our early experience
2. Developmentalists with a **change** perspective believe that we often develop into someone different from who we were at an earlier point in development

3

V. **Sociocultural contexts** of development
  A. **Context** is the setting in which development occurs, a setting that is influenced by historical, economic, social, and cultural factors
  B. **Culture** is the behavior patterns, beliefs, and all other products of a particular group of people that are passed on from generation to generation
  C. **Ethnicity** is based on cultural heritage, nationality characteristics, race, religion, and language
    1. **Ethnic identity** is a sense of membership based on the shared language, religion, customs, values, history, and race of an ethnic group
    2. There is **diversity** within each ethnic group; groups should not be considered homogeneous
    3. Ethnic minority populations are increasing in the United States
  D. **Gender** is the sociocultural dimension of being female or male
    1. **Sex** refers to the biological dimension of being female or male
    2. Society's gender attitudes have changed over the years
VI. **Genetics**
  A. **General information**
    1. Principles of **genetics** explain the mechanisms for transmitting characteristics from one generation to the next
    2. Everyone carries a genetic code inherited from their parents
    3. The genetic code is carried by biochemical agents called genes and chromosomes which are located within the cells of the body
    4. Encoded within the genes and chromosomes are the instructions that direct the development that occurs as individuals go from a single cell into an adult made of trillions of cells
  B. **Chromosomes**
    1. Chromosomes are threadlike structures that come in structurally similar pairs and contain deoxyribonucleic acid (DNA)
    2. DNA contains genetic information
    3. 46 chromosomes (23 pairs) in each human cell
      a. **22 pairs of autosomal chromosomes:** Each member of an autosomal pair looks alike even though they may carry different genetic information
      b. **One pair of sex chromosomes:** They do not necessarily look alike
        (1) Males have one X chromosome and one Y chromosome
        (2) Females have two X chromosomes
        (3) The sex chromosomes contain genes that control the development of primary and secondary sex characteristics and various sex-linked traits
        (4) The Y chromosome is physically smaller than the X chromosome and, therefore, carries fewer genes than the X chromosome
    4. One member of each chromosomal pair came from each parent
  C. **Genes**
    1. Genes are segments of chromosomes
    2. Each chromosome contains tens of thousands of genes
    3. There are about one million genes on all 46 chromosomes
    4. Genes are made of DNA
    5. Act as blueprints for cells to reproduce themselves and produce the proteins that maintain life
  D. **Genetic principles**
    1. **Dominant-recessive principle**
      a. If one gene of a pair is dominant and one is recessive, the dominant gene exerts its effect, overriding the potential influence of the other, recessive gene
      b. A recessive gene exerts its influence only if the two genes of a pair are both recessive
      c. An example of a trait that follows a dominant-recessive pattern of inheritance is eye color

4

2. **Sex-linked traits:** Some characteristics are determined by genes carried on the sex chromosomes with the result that these characteristics are more or less likely to appear in members of one sex (e.g., color blindness, hemophilia)
3. **Polygenic inheritance:** The interaction of many genes produce a particular characteristic (e.g. height)
4. **Genotype** is a person's genetic heritage, the actual genetic material
5. **Phenotype** is the way an individual's genotype is expressed in observed and measurable characteristics
6. **Reaction range** is used to describe the range of phenotypes for each genotype, suggesting the importance of an environment's restrictiveness or enrichment
7. **Canalization** describes the narrow path or developmental course that certain characteristics take; preservative forces help to protect or buffer a person from environmental extremes

E. **Cell reproduction**
1. **Mitosis**
   a. Involves the duplication of a cell
   b. The process of ordinary cell division that results in two cells
   c. Each cell produced has 46 chromosomes, identical to those in the parent cell
2. **Meiosis**
   a. Involves the halving of a cell for reproduction
   b. Meiosis is the process through which genes are transmitted from parents to offspring
   c. In meiosis, each pair of chromosomes in a cell separates, and one member of each pair goes into each gamete, or "offspring" cell
   d. Each reproductive cell has 23 unpaired chromosomes (1/2 of the genetic material of the parent)

Prenatal Development and Birth Review

I. **Human reproduction**
   A. **Gametes** are human reproductive cells, which are created in the testes of males and the ovaries of females
   B. Gametes are formed by meiosis
   C. Female gametes are called **ovum**
   D. Male gametes are called **sperm**
   E. **Conception** takes place when the ovum is fertilized by a single sperm
   F. Usually occurs in the fallopian tube
   G. Fertilized ovum is called a **zygote**
   H. Reproductive technology, such as **in vitro fertilization**, wherein conception occurs outside the body, is sometimes used when couples have fertility problems

II. **Gestation**
   A. **Gestation**, the developmental time spent in utero, lasts for 9 calendar months or 10 lunar months or 40 weeks
   B. Gestation is divided into three **trimesters**
      1. **First trimester** refers to the first 3 months of pregnancy
      2. **Second trimester** refers to the middle 3 months of pregnancy
      3. **Third trimester** refers to the last 3 months of pregnancy

III. **Periods of prenatal development**
   A. **Germinal period**
      1. Germinal period begins with conception and lasts until 2 weeks after conception
      2. Zygote undergoes rapid cell division
      3. One week after conception, differentiation of cells has occurred as inner and outer layers of the organism are formed
         a. The **blastocyst** is the inner layer of cells that develops; it is shaped like a hollow ball; it later develops into the embryo
         b. The **trophoblast** is the outer layer of cells that develops; it later turns into the placenta which provides nutritional support for the embryo
      4. Blastocyst attaches to the uterine wall 6-7 days after conception
      5. Blastocyst is completely embedded in the uterine wall 10-15 days after conception
      6. End of the germinal period is marked by the implantation of the blastocyst into the uterine wall
   B. **Embryonic period**
      1. Embryonic period covers the period from 2 to 8 weeks after conception
      2. Developing organism is called an **embryo** during this period
      3. Growth during prenatal development follows a **cephalocaudal** (from head to tail) and **proximodistal** (from center to extremities) pattern
      4. **Embryo differentiates into three layers**
         a. **Ectoderm:** Outermost layer, which will become the skin parts (such as hair and nails), the nervous system, and sensory receptors (such as eyes, ears, nose, and mouth)
         b. **Mesoderm:** Middle layer, which will develop into the circulatory system, bones, muscle, excretory system, and reproductive system
         c. **Endoderm:** Inner layer, which will turn into the digestive and respiratory systems
      5. The formation of organs, called **organogenesis**, takes place
         a. **Neural tube** forms at 3 weeks
         b. **Eyes** begin to appear at 21 days
         c. **Heart** cells differentiate at 24 days
         d. **Arm and leg buds** appear and differentiate at 26 to 28 days
         e. About 95% of the body parts have appeared by the end of the embryonic period
      6. **Life-support systems** for the embryo develop
         a. **Amnion**
            (1) A fluid-filled sac that forms around the embryo
            (2) Functions as a shock absorber
         b. **Placenta**
            (1) A mass of tissue containing intertwined but unconnected blood vessels from the mother and embryo
            (2) Also called **afterbirth**
            (3) Functions include respiration, nutrition, excretion, and protection
         c. **Umbilical cord**
            (1) Connects the embryo to the placenta
            (2) Contains two arteries and one vein
            (3) Blood from placenta brings food oxygen, hormones, and protective antibodies to embryo via umbilical vein
      7. At 8 weeks, embryo is a little more than 1 inch long and weighs about 1/30 of an ounce; head takes up approximately 1/2 of the total body length
      8. At the end of the embryonic period, cartilage is replaced by the first bone cells

C. **Fetal period**
  1. Fetal period goes from 8 weeks after conception until birth
  2. Developing organism is now called a **fetus**
  3. During this period there is a **substantial increase in fetal size**
  4. Structures formed during the embryonic period grow, elaborate, and begin to function
  5. **Growth**
    a. ₃ months
      (1) About 3 inches long and weighs about one ounce
      (2) Facial features are distinguishable
      (3) Genitals can be identified as male or female
      (4) Fetus moves body parts
      (5) Swallows
      (6) Fetal heart audible
    b. **4 months**
      (1) 5 1/2 inches long and weighs about 4 ounces
      (2) Fetal movements can be felt for the first time by the mother at about 4 months, called **quickening**
      (3) **Vernix** (a cheesy material that protects the skin), and **lanugo** (downy hair) cover fetus
    c. **5 months**
      (1) 10 to 12 inches long and weighs 1/2 to 1 pound
      (2) Toenails and fingernails have formed
      (3) Hair growth on head, eyelashes, eyebrows
      (4) Eyes fused shut
    d. **6 months**
      (1) 14 inches long and weighs 1 1/2 to 2 pounds
      (2) Eyes and eyelids are completely formed; eyelids open
    e. **7 months**
      (1) 14 to 17 inches long and weighs 2 1/2 to 3 pounds
      (2) Lungs produce surfactants
    f. **8th and 9th months**
      (1) More fat deposits are laid down
      (2) Gains another 4 pounds
      (3) At birth, the average baby is 20 inches long and weighs 7 to 7 1/2 pounds

IV. **Teratogens**
  A. A **teratogen** is any agent that causes a birth defect
  B. **Effects of exposure to teratogens vary depending on the prenatal period**
    1. **Germinal period**: An all or nothing effect
      a. Prenatal death
      b. No damage
    2. **Embryonic period**: Results in major structural abnormalities because this is when organs are being formed
      a. Brain most vulnerable at 15 to 25 days after conception
      b. Eye most susceptible at 24 to 40 days after conception
      c. Heart most likely to be damaged from 20 to 40 days
      d. Legs most vulnerable at 24 to 36 days
    3. **Fetal period**: Affects growth
      a. Stunts growth
      b. Creates problems in the way organs function

C. **Specific teratogens**
  1. **Maternal diseases** can cause damage by crossing the placental barrier during pregnancy or by causing damage during the birth process
      a. **Rubella** (German measles)
        (1) Greatest damage when mothers contract rubella during the 3rd and 4th weeks of pregnancy although can cause damage through the 2nd month of pregnancy
        (2) Can cause mental retardation, blindness, deafness, and heart problems
      b. **Syphilis**
        (1) A sexually transmitted disease
        (2) More damaging later in pregnancy -- 4 months or more after conception
        (3) Damages organs after they form
        (4) Can cause eye lesions that lead to blindness and skin lesions
        (5) Can cause problems with the central nervous system and gastrointestinal tract
      c. **Genital herpes**
        (1) Can be transmitted to newborns during delivery through the birth canal when the mother has an active case of genital herpes
        (2) About 1/3 of babies die
        (3) About 1/4 become brain damaged
        (4) Delivery by cesarean section prevents the virus from infecting the newborn
      d. **Acquired immune deficiency syndrome (AIDS)**
        (1) A sexually transmitted disease caused by a virus that destroys the body's immune system
        (2) AIDS can be transmitted to offspring
          (a) During gestation, across the placenta
          (b) During delivery, through contact with maternal blood or fluids
          (c) Postpartum, though breast-feeding
        (3) About 1/3 of infants born to mothers with AIDS will develop the HIV virus
  2. **Other maternal factors**
      a. **Maternal age**
        (1) **Adolescent mothers**
          (a) More often have premature babies
          (b) Higher mortality rate of infants
          (c) Factors related to increased problems include immature reproductive system, poor nutrition, lack of prenatal care, and low socioeconomic status
        (2) **Older mothers**
          (a) Older mothers have a higher risk of having infants with Down Syndrome and other genetic disorders
          (b) Women in their mid- to late-thirties or forties are more likely to experience fertility problems than women in their twenties
          (c) The older the mother is, the higher the risk of genetic disorders and infertility
      b. **Nutrition**
        (1) Total number of calories and sufficient levels of protein, vitamins, and minerals are important for fetal health
        (2) Mothers with poor diets are more likely to have infants who weigh less, have less vitality, and are born prematurely
      c. **Stress**
        (1) Can cause physiological changes in the mother such as increased respiration and glandular secretions, may deprive fetus of adequate oxygen
        (2) Anxiety during pregnancy is associated with increased crying and activity in infants

3. **Drugs**
   a. **Alcohol**
      (1) **Fetal alcohol syndrome** is a cluster of abnormalities that appear in the offspring of mothers who drink alcohol heavily during pregnancy
      (2) Infant abnormalities include facial deformities, defective limbs, face, and heart
      (3) Most infants are below average in intelligence and some are mentally retarded
   b. **Tobacco**
      (1) Cigarette smoking during pregnancy is associated with higher rates of fetal and neonatal deaths
      (2) Higher incidence of preterm births and low birthweight babies
      (3) Respiratory problems and sudden infant death syndrome (SIDS) more common
   c. **Marijuana**
      (1) Use during pregnancy is related to increased tremors and startles among newborns
      (2) Associated with poorer verbal and memory development at 4 years of age
   d. **Heroin**
      (1) Infants born to mothers addicted to heroin are born addicted themselves
      (2) Signs of withdrawal shown by infants after birth
         (a) Tremors
         (b) Irritability
         (c) Abnormal crying
         (d) Disturbed sleep
         (e) Impaired motor control
      (3) May show attention deficits later in childhood
   e. **Cocaine**
      (1) Mothers who use cocaine during pregnancy are more likely to have infants with low birthweight and reduced length
      (2) Increased incidence of other congenital abnormalities, but this may also be due to other factors such as malnutrition and other substance abuse that are commonly found in cocaine users
   f. **Diethylstilbestrol (DES)**
      (1) A drug often prescribed for women who were at risk for spontaneous abortions during the 1940s through the 1960s
      (2) Increased incidence of vaginal cancer has been found in daughters of women who took DES while they were pregnant
   g. **Thalidomide**
      (1) A popular tranquilizer in the early 1960s used to alleviate morning sickness
      (2) Caused deformities in limbs, depending on time during pregnancy it was taken
4. **Environmental hazards**
   a. **Radiation**
      (1) Can cause genetic mutations
      (2) Increased incidence of chromosomal abnormalities in children whose fathers were exposed to high levels of radiation before conception
      (3) Most dangerous time to developing embryo and fetus is in the first several weeks after conception
      (4) Pregnant women should avoid X rays
   b. **Pollutants**
      (1) Dangerous pollutants include carbon monoxide, mercury, and lead
      (2) Prenatal exposure to lead is associated with decreased mental development
      (3) Pregnant women exposed to PCB's have an increased risk of having smaller, preterm infants

        c. **Toxoplasmosis**
           (1) A mild infection that causes cold-like symptoms or no apparent illness in adults
           (2) Can be a teratogen during prenatal development
           (3) Cats are common carriers of toxoplasmosis, especially outdoor cats
           (4) Eating raw or undercooked meat can also cause toxoplasmosis
           (5) May cause eye defects, brain defects, and premature birth
        d. **Prolonged exposure to heat in hot tubs or saunas**
           (1) May raise the mother's body temperature
           (2) May interfere with cell division and cause birth defects or fetal death
           (3) Pregnant women should spend no more than 10 minutes in a sauna or hot tub

V. **Genetic and chromosomal abnormalities**
  A. **Phenylketonuria (PKU)**
    1. A genetic disorder in which the individual cannot properly metabolize protein
    2. Easily detected by a blood test
    3. Can be treated by a diet in which the individual avoids products containing phenylalanine
    4. If not treated, results in mental retardation and hyperactivity
  B. **Down syndrome**
    1. The most common genetically transmitted form of mental retardation
    2. Caused by the presence of an extra (47th) chromosome
    3. Results in characteristic physical traits, including a broad, flat face and oval, upward-slanting eyes
    4. Associated with mild to severe mental retardation
  C. **Sickle-cell anemia**
    1. A genetic disorder caused by a recessive gene
    2. Affects red blood cells, changing its shape to a hook-shaped "sickle"
    3. Causes anemia and early death because of failure to carry oxygen to the body's cells
    4. Occurs most often in African-Americans
  D. **Klinefelter syndrome**
    1. A genetic disorder in which males have an extra X chromosome, making them XXY instead of XY
    2. Associated with abnormally small testes after puberty, low levels of testosterone, and above average height
  E. **Turner syndrome**
    1. A genetic disorder in which females are missing an X chromosome, making them XO instead of XX
    2. These females are often short in height and have a webbed neck and may have a cognitive defect in perceptual organization
  F. **XYY syndrome**
    1. A genetic disorder in which a male has an extra Y chromosome
    2. In the past, it was believed that these males were overly aggressive and violent but this has not been supported by more recent research

VI. **Prenatal diagnostic tests**
  A. **Amniocentesis**
    1. After 15 to 18 weeks a sample of amniotic fluid is withdrawn by syringe
    2. Fluid is tested to detect chromosomal or metabolic disorders and to determine sex
  B. **Ultrasound**
    1. High frequency sound waves are directed into the pregnant woman's abdomen in order to get a visual representation of the fetal structures
    2. Can be used to identify multiple pregnancies, structural abnormalities, and to determine gestational age and fetal position

C. **Chorionic villus sampling**
   1. A small sample of the placenta is removed at some point between the 8th and the 11th week of pregnancy; can be performed earlier than amniocentesis
   2. Used to determine whether there are any genetic abnormalities
D. **Alpha-fetoprotein test**:
   1. A blood test
   2. Used to assess alphaprotein level which is associated with neural tube defects

VII. **Birth**
A. **Stages of birth**
   1. **First stage**
      a. Begins with uterine contractions, about 15 to 20 minutes apart
      b. Contractions cause cervix to open
      c. Contractions become progressively stronger and closer together, until they are about 2 to 5 minutes apart
      d. By the end of the first stage, the cervix is dilated to about 4 inches
      e. First stage lasts an average of 12 to 24 hours
   2. **Second stage**
      a. Begins when the baby's head moves through the cervix and into the birth canal
      b. Ends when the baby is out of the mother's body
      c. Mother bears down and pushes the baby out during this stage
      d. Contractions come about every minute and last for about one minute
      e. Second stage lasts about 1 1/2 hours
   3. **Third stage**
      a. This stage is sometimes called **afterbirth**
      b. The placenta, umbilical cord, and other membranes are detached and expelled
      c. Shortest of the stages, lasts only a few minutes
B. **Use of drugs during childbirth**
   1. Tranquilizers, sedatives, and analgesics are often used to relieve pain
   2. Medications may cross the placental barrier and affect the fetus
   3. The use of medication should be kept to a minimum
   4. **Oxytocin**
      a. A hormone that stimulates and regulates the rhythmicity of uterine contractions, has been widely used as a drug to speed delivery
      b. Can save the mother's life or keep baby being damaged by prolonged delivery
      c. Problems include infants who are more likely to have jaundice and an increased likelihood of mother needing painkilling drugs
C. **Delivery complications**
   1. **Precipitate delivery**
      a. A delivery that takes place too rapidly, that is, the baby takes less than 10 minutes to be squeezed through the birth canal
      b. Can cause disturbed blood flow in the infant and hemorrhaging
   2. **Anoxia**
      a. Insufficient supply of oxygen to the infant
      b. Can happen when delivery takes too long
      c. Can cause brain damage in the infant
   3. **Breech position**
      a. Occurs when the baby's position in the uterus is such that the buttocks are the first part to emerge from the vagina
      b. Because the baby's head is still in the uterus when the rest of the body is out, respiratory problems may result
      c. Some babies in a breech position are delivered by cesarean section

4. **Cesarean section**
   a. The surgical removal of the baby from the uterus
   b. Reasons for a cesarean section
      (1) Baby in a breech position or lying crosswise in the uterus
      (2) Baby's head is too large to pass through the mother's pelvis
      (3) Baby develops complications
      (4) Mother is bleeding vaginally
   c. Cesarean sections can be safer than some risky deliveries, such as when the baby is in a breech position, but are associated with a higher infection rate, longer hospital stay, and greater expense
   d. Rates of cesarean sections increased during the 1980s but are now slowing down

VIII. **The postpartal period**
   A. **Postpartal period**
      1. Period after childbirth or delivery
      2. Time when the woman adjusts, both physically and psychologically, to the process of childbearing
      3. Lasts for about 6 weeks or until the body has completed its adjustment and has returned to a near prepregnant state
   B. **Physical adjustments**
      1. Most feel tired and need rest, but some may have a great deal of energy
      2. Fatigue can interfere with feelings of ability to care for baby
      3. **Involution** is the process by which the uterus returns to its prepregnant size 5 or 6 weeks after birth
      4. After delivery, estrogen and progesterone levels drop sharply and stay low until ovaries start producing hormones again
      5. Menstruation usually begins again 4 to 8 weeks after delivery if not breast-feeding; may be several months before menstruation starts if breastfeeding
      6. Usually recommended to wait until 6 weeks after birth to have sexual intercourse
      7. Exercise is recommended during the postpartal period to help woman regain body shape
   C. **Emotional and psychological adjustments**
      1. **Emotional fluctuations**
         a. Emotional fluctuations common due to hormonal changes, fatigue, inexperience with babies, or because of demands involved in caring for a newborn
         b. May last only a few weeks or much longer
         c. Signs that indicate professional counseling may be needed
            (1) Excessive worrying
            (2) Depression
            (3) Extreme changes in appetite
            (4) Crying spells
            (5) Inability to sleep
      2. **Adjusting to becoming a competent parent**
         a. Mother and father need to become aware of infant's physical, psychological, and emotional developmental needs
         b. **Bonding** refers to the occurrence of close contact, especially physical, between parents and newborn in the period shortly after birth
      3. **Adjustments in the marital relationship**
         a. Determining responsibilities for new parenting demands
         b. Finding time for each other
         c. Deciding on priorities

4. **Deciding whether to work or not**
   a. A dilemma for many women
   b. Factors considered when making the decision
      (1) Deciding on priorities as they concern family, baby, career, finances, luxuries
      (2) Personality factors
      (3) Substitute caregiver arrangements
      (4) Energy and stamina available and needed
      (5) Possible stress caused by conflicting job and family roles
      (6) Support available from baby's father, other family members
      (7) Financial needs
      (8) Job flexibility, influence on career path

Introduction to Development and Prenatal Development Review Questions

Medea, a 25-year-old female, is 8 weeks pregnant with her first child. She is talking to the clinic nurse during her first prenatal visit.

Questions 1-7 refer to the above situation.

1. In which trimester of pregnancy is Medea?
   a. first
   b. second
   c. third
   d. fourth

2. If Medea carries her baby full-term, about how many more weeks does she have before her baby is born?
   a. 18
   b. 22
   c. 28
   d. 32

3. Medea is concerned because she has not yet felt her baby move. What could the nurse tell her about when to expect to first feel her baby move (quickening)?
   a. She should have felt the baby move as soon as conception occurred.
   b. Fetal movement is usually felt by the mother for the first time at about two months, so Medea should be feeling movement any day now.
   c. Fetal movement is not usually felt by the mother until about 4 months.
   d. Fetal movement is not usually felt by the mother until about 6 months.

4. Medea has a history of genetic disorders in her family and wants to find out as soon as possible whether her baby has any genetic or chromosomal abnormalities. Which of the following procedures would be most appropriate?
   a. Ultrasound
   b. Amniocentesis
   c. Chorionic villus sampling
   d. Alpha-fetoprotein test

5. Medea has genital herpes and is worried about how this will affect her baby. What can the nurse tell her about the dangers of genital herpes during pregnancy and birth?
   a. If Medea has an active case of genital herpes at the time of delivery, having a cesarean section would prevent the virus from infecting her child.
   b. Genital herpes typically causes organ malformations early in pregnancy.
   c. Most babies born to mothers with genital herpes die.
   d. Genital herpes cannot be passed on to offspring during pregnancy or birth.

6. Medea enjoys relaxing in a hot tub, but wonders if she should continue doing so while she is pregnant. What can the nurse tell her about using hot tubs while pregnant?
   a. Relaxing in a hot tub can be a great stress reliever and is often recommended during pregnancy.
   b. Relaxing in a hot tub for more than 10 minutes at a time can raise the mother's body temperature and cause birth defects or fetal death.
   c. As long as Medea was a regular user of hot tubs before she became pregnant, she can continue to use the hot tub with no restrictions.
   d. Prolonged exposure to heat while in a hot tub is only dangerous during the last trimester of pregnancy.

7. Medea has been discussing child rearing with her husband. He says development is totally determined by the genes, so what they do doesn't really matter. She thinks the way children are reared determines how they turn out. What is the prevailing thought on the nature-nurture controversy?
   a. Nature (genes) is the primary influence on the developmental outcome.
   b. Nurture (environment) is the sole determinant of developmental outcome.
   c. Both nature and nurture interact to determine the developmental outcome.
   d. Controversial issues should not be discussed during pregnancy.

8. Which of the following is NOT one of the characteristics of a life-span approach to development?
   a. Development occurs in the biological, cognitive, and social domains.
   b. Development is influenced by historical conditions.
   c. Developmental gains occur until early adulthood and then losses begin.
   d. Development is studied by a number of different disciplines.

9. Changes that occur in an individual's thought, intelligence, and language are referred to as
   a. socioemotional changes
   b. cognitive changes
   c. biological changes
   d. normative changes

10. Each human cell, with the exception of human reproductive cells, contains
    a. 46 chromosomes
    b. 44 chromosomes
    c. 23 chromosomes
    d. 22 chromosomes

11. The process by which cells are halved in order to transmit genes from parents to offspring is called
    a. meiosis
    b. mitosis
    c. organogenesis
    d. polygenic inheritance

12. Conception occurs at the beginning of the _____ period of prenatal development.
    a. fetal
    b. embryonic
    c. organogenesis
    d. germinal

13. The embryo differentiates into three layers. The outermost layer, which will become the skin parts, the nervous system, and sensory receptors is called the
    a. mesoderm
    b. ectoderm
    c. medoderm
    d. endoderm

14. The embryo receives nourishment from the mother via the placenta and the
    a. amnion
    b. chorion
    c. endoderm
    d. umbilical cord

15. During prenatal development, most organs are formed during
    a. the germinal period
    b. conception
    c. the embryonic period
    d. the fetal period

16. During the fetal period,
    a. the blastocyst develops
    b. organogenesis occurs
    c. there is substantial growth
    d. implantation occurs

17. Growth during prenatal development follows a cephalocaudal pattern which means that it proceeds from
    a. bottom to top
    b. top to bottom
    c. the center to the extremities
    d. the extremities to the center

18. The developing individual is referred to as an embryo from
    a. conception to birth
    b. conception to 2 weeks after conception
    c. 2 to 8 weeks after conception
    d. 8 weeks after conception to birth

19. The term **teratogen** refers to
    a. a cheesy material that protects fetal skin
    b. downy hair that covers a fetus
    c. an agent that causes a birth defect
    d. an insufficient supply of oxygen to the infant during birth

20. Which prenatal diagnostic procedure involves using sound waves in order to get a visual representation of the fetal structures?
    a. alpha-fetoprotein test
    b. amniocentesis
    c. chorionic villus sampling
    d. ultrasound

21. Which prenatal diagnostic procedure is used primarily to detect neural tube defects?
    a. alpha-fetoprotein test
    b. amniocentesis
    c. chorionic villus sampling
    d. ultrasound

22. During which period of prenatal development are teratogens most likely to either have no effect or to result in fetal death?
    a. fetal
    b. embryonic
    c. terminal
    d. germinal

23. Compared to women in their twenties, teenage mothers
    a. have lower rates of infant mortality
    b. are less likely to have premature babies
    c. are less likely to have good prenatal care and nutrition
    d. have similar rates of infant mortality, premature babies, and prenatal care

24. Sickle-cell anemia is most common among
    a. African-Americans
    b. European-Americans
    c. Hispanics
    d. Native Americans

25. Phenylketonuria (PKU) is
    a. a genetic disorder in which males have an extra X chromosome
    b. a genetic disorder in which females are missing an X chromosome
    c. a genetic disorder that can be detected by a blood test and controlled by diet
    d. the most common genetically transmitted form of mental retardation

26. Noriko is in the third stage of childbirth. Which of the following should be taking place at this time?
    a. the beginning of contractions, about 15 to 20 minutes apart
    b. the movement of the baby's head into the birth canal
    c. bearing down and pushing the baby out
    d. the detachment and expulsion of the placenta

27. Which is usually the longest stage of childbirth?
    a. the first stage
    b. the second stage
    c. the third stage
    d. the fourth stage

28. Gabrielle is having a precipitate delivery. That means she is having
    a. a premature infant
    b. a delivery that takes place too rapidly
    c. a disruption in the oxygen supply to the infant
    d. her baby surgically removed from her uterus

29. Sophia is having a breech baby. Which part of the baby is presenting first?
    a. the head
    b. the arms
    c. the buttocks
    d. the shoulder

30. Oxytocin is a drug that
    a. is often used to speed delivery during birth
    b. was often given to pregant women in the 1950s and 60s that is associated with vaginal cancer in their daughters
    c. is used to relieve pain during childbirth
    d. is used to treat genetic disorders

Introduction to Development and Prenatal Development Review Answers

1. a
2. d
3. c
4. c
5. a
6. b
7. c
8. c
9. b
10. a
11. a
12. d
13. b
14. d
15. c
16. c
17. b
18. c
19. c
20. d
21. a
22. d
23. c
24. a
25. c
26. d
27. a
28. b
29. c
30. a

SECTION III   INFANCY AND TODDLERHOOD CONCEPT REVIEW
   (0 TO 2 YEARS)

I. **Physical development**
   A. **Infant classifications**
      1. **Full term** if born 38 to 42 weeks after conception
      2. **Preterm** if born less than 37 weeks after conception
      3. **Postterm** if born more than 42 weeks after conception
      4. **Low-birthweight** if born after a normal gestation period but weighs less than 5 1/2 pounds (2.5 kilograms)
   B. **Preterm and low-birthweight infants**
      1. Both preterm and low birthweight infants are considered high risk infants
      2. Prematurity does not necessarily harm infants but puts them at higher risk for having physical and mental problems
      3. As technology has improved, the serious consequences of preterm birth have decreased
      4. Preterm infants born with a problem that is identifiable at birth are likely to have a poorer developmental future than preterm infants born without a recognizable problem
      5. Extremely tiny and extremely early infants are most likely to have a poorer developmental future
      6. Social class differences are related to preterm infants' development; the higher the SES, the more favorable the developmental outcome
      7. Social class differences are related to other variables that affect development with lower SES environments more likely to involve tobacco and alcohol consumption, lower IQ of parents, and less knowledge of competent parenting strategies
   C. **Infant states and sleep**
      1. **Classifications**
         a. Deep sleep
         b. Regular sleep
         c. Disturbed sleep
         d. Drowsy
         e. Alert activity
         f. Alert and focused
         g. Inflexibly focused
      2. **About sleep**
         a. Newborns sleep for an average of 16 to 17 hours a day; normal range is from 10 to 21 hours
         b. Newborn sleep does not always follow a rhythmic pattern
         c. Amount of time spent sleeping gradually decreases
         d. By 4 months, sleep longest at night and have the longest span of being awake during the day
      3. **Sudden infant death syndrome (SIDS)**
         a. A condition that occurs when an infant stops breathing, usually during the night while sleeping, and suddenly dies without apparent cause
         b. Leading cause of death for infants 10 days to 1 year of age
         c. Occurs most often between 2 and 4 months; 90% occur by 6 months
         d. **Risk factors for SIDS**
            (1)   Prematurity
            (2)   Low birthweight
            (3)   Low Apgar scores
            (4)   Respiratory problems
            (5)   Infants sleeping on abdomens
            (6)   Infants using soft pillows or mattresses
            (7)   Males

D. **Infant reflexes**
  1. Automatic responses to certain stimuli
  2. Indicate the integrity of the nervous system; if they fail to appear or disappear at the appropriate time can indicate a problem
  3. Involuntary behaviors that are replaced by voluntary behaviors as the infant gets older
  4. **Specific reflexes**
     a. **Babinski**
        (1) Stimulation: Sole of foot stroked
        (2) Infant's response: Fans out toes, twists foot in
        (3) Developmental pattern: Disappears 9 months to 1 year
     b. **Blinking**
        (1) Stimulation: Flash of light, puff of air
        (2) Infant's response: Closes both eyes
        (3) Developmental pattern: Permanent
     c. **Gag**
        (1) Stimulation: Food, suction or passage of tube touching posterior pharynx
        (2) Infant's response: Causes gagging
        (3) Developmental pattern: Permanent
     d. **Grasping**
        (1) Stimulation: Palms touched
        (2) Infant's response: Grasps tightly
        (3) Developmental pattern: Weakens after 3 months, disappears after 1 year
     e. **Moro** (startle)
        (1) Stimulation: Sudden stimulation, such as hearing loud noise or being dropped
        (2) Infant's response: Startles, arches back, throws head back, flings out arms and legs and then rapidly closes them to center of body
        (3) Developmental pattern: Disappears 3 to 4 months
     f. **Rooting**
        (1) Stimulation: Cheek stroked or side of mouth touched
        (2) Infant's response: Turns head, opens mouth, begins sucking
        (3) Developmental pattern: Disappears 3 to 4 months
     g. **Stepping**
        (1) Stimulation: Infant held above surface and feet lowered to touch surface
        (2) Infant's response: Moves feet as if to walk
        (3) Developmental pattern: Disappears 3 to 4 months
     h. **Sucking**
        (1) Stimulation: Object touching mouth
        (2) Infant's response: Sucks automatically
        (3) Developmental pattern: Disappears 3 to 4 months
     i. **Swimming**
        (1) Stimulation: Infant put face down in water
        (2) Infant's response: Makes coordinated swimming movements
        (3) Developmental pattern: Disappears 6 to 7 months
     j. **Tonic neck**
        (1) Stimulation: Infant placed on back
        (2) Infant's response: Forms fists with both hands and usually turns head to the right (sometimes called the "fencer's pose" because the infant looks like it is assuming a fencer's position)
        (3) Developmental pattern: Disappears 2 months

E. **Growth** continues to follow a cephalocaudal and proximodistal pattern
1. **Height**
   a. **At birth**, the average newborn is 20 inches (50.8 centimeters) long; 95% are between 18 (45.7 centimeters) and 22 inches (55.9 centimeters) in length
   b. Growth is very rapid during the first year of life
   c. During the first year, infants grow about 1 inch per month
   d. **By one year**, they are about 1 1/2 times their birth length
   e. Growth slows down during the second year of life
   f. **By two years**, the average infant is 32 to 35 inches in height
   g. Height at two years is almost 1/2 of their adult height
2. **Weight**
3. **At birth**, the average newborn weighs 7 1/2 pounds (3.4 kilograms); 95% weigh between 5 1/2 (2.5 kilograms) and 10 pounds (4.5 kilograms)
4. During the first few days after birth, infants lose 5 to 7% of their body weight as they adjust to feeding
5. After the first few days, they gain an average of 5 to 6 ounces per week during the first month of life
6. By 5 months, birthweight is doubled
7. **By one year**, birthweight is tripled
8. During the second year, they gain 1/4 to 1/2 of a pound per month
9. **By two years**, the average toddler weighs 26 to 32 pounds
10. Weight at two years is about 1/5 of their adult weight

F. **Fontanels**
1. Posterior fontanel closed by 6 to 8 weeks
2. Anterior fontanel remains open through first 12 months; usually closed by 18 months

G. **Teething**
1. Generally begins around 6 months
2. First two teeth are the two lower central incisors
3. By one year, infants have 6 to 8 teeth
4. By two years, about 16 teeth

H. **Gross motor skills**
1. **Gross motor skills** involve large muscle activities such as moving one's arms and walking
2. Motor milestones can vary as much as 2 to 4 months among normal infants, especially those that occur at later ages
3. The sequence in which the milestones occur is the same for most infants
4. **1 month**
   a. Lifts head while in a prone position
   b. Turns head from side to side
   c. Reflexes dominate behavior
5. **2 to 3 months**
   a. Lifts chest using arms for support in a prone position
   b. Bears some weight on legs when held in a standing position
6. **4 to 5 months**
   a. Balances head well
   b. Can sit when well-supported
   c. Rolls from abdomen to back
   d. Primitive reflexes have disappeared
7. **6 to 7 months**
   a. Sits without support
   b. Turns over from stomach or back
   c. Plays with feet, puts them in mouth

19

8. **8 to 9 months**
   a. Crawls
   b. Pulls up to a standing position
   c. Stands while holding on to furniture
9. **10 to 11 months**
   a. Begins **cruising**, which is walking using furniture for support
   b. Stands alone for short periods of time
   c. Sits down from a standing position without help
10. **12 to 13 months**
    a. Walks without assistance
11. **15 to 18 months**
    a. Pulls toy on a string while walking
    b. Climbs stairs using hands and legs
    c. Rides four-wheel vehicles
    d. Walks well alone
    e. Drinks from cup
    f. Uses spoon
12. **18 to 24 months**
    a. Walks fast and runs stiffly
    b. Balances on feet in a squat position while playing with toys
    c. Walks backwards without losing balance
    d. Stands and kicks a ball without falling
    e. Stands and throws a ball
    f. Jumps in place
    g. Climbs stairs well
    h. During the second year toddlers become more mobile
    i. Motor activity at this time is important for development and should not be restricted other than for safety reasons

I. **Fine motor skills**
   1. **Fine motor skills** involve finely turned movements such as finger dexterity
   2. **Birth:** Infants have little control over fine motor skills
   3. **2 to 3 months**
      a. Holds rattle but will not reach for it
      b. Plays with fingers and hands
   4. **4 to 5 months**
      a. Reaches for object with whole hand
      b. Misjudges distances when reaching
      c. Brings object to mouth
   5. **6 to 7 months**
      a. Transfers an object from one hand to another
      b. Reaches for toy and grasps it with one hand
   6. **8 to 9 months**
      a. Uses a pincer grasp
      b. Reaching and grasping become more refined over the first two years of life
   7. **10 to 12 months**
      a. Can hold a crayon to make a mark on a piece of paper
   8. **15 months**
      a. Builds a tower of 2 blocks
   9. **18 months**
      a. Builds a tower of 3 to 4 blocks

10. **24 months**
    a. Builds a tower of 6 to 7 blocks

J. **The senses**
  1. **Vision**
    a. Newborn vision is about 20/200 to 20/600 on the Snellen chart
    b. At birth, infants prefer to look at patterns rather than color or brightness
    c. By 6 months, vision is 20/100 or better
    d. By 6 months, infants can perceive depth
  2. **Hearing**
    a. Hearing begins prenatally; fetuses are able to hear sounds during the last few months before birth
    b. Newborns' hearing sensory thresholds are higher than adults, so a sound must be louder to be heard by a newborn than by an adult
  3. **Touch**
    a. Newborns respond to touch
    b. Newborns can feel pain
  4. **Smell**
    a. Newborn infants can distinguish between odors
    b. Young infants display preferences for certain odors
  5. **Taste**
    a. Prenatal sensitivity to taste has been demonstrated
    b. Newborns show a preference for sweet tastes
    c. Newborns display sensitivity to sour tastes

K. **Nutritional needs**
  1. Infants use about 50 calories per day for each pound they weigh, more than twice the adult requirement per pound
  2. Breast-feeding is better than bottle feeding better for the baby's health, and is recommended for the first 4 to 6 months of life
  3. Breastmilk is easily digestible and helps immunize the newborn from disease
  4. Solids should be started at about 6 months
  5. First solids should be strained, pureed, or finely mashed
  6. Finger foods such as toast or teething crackers can be introduced at about 6 or 7 months
  7. Chopped table food or junior foods can be started by 9 to 12 months
  8. Weaning from bottle or breast to cup should occur gradually, usually starting in second half of first year

L. **Toilet training**
  1. Toilet training is generally expected to be attained by 3 years of age
  2. The trend today is to begin toilet training later than in the past
  3. Toilet training typically begins at about 20 months to 2 years
  4. Length of time to master the skill varies with each child
  5. Prerequisites for toilet training include appropriate muscular maturation, cognitive maturity, and motivation
  6. Toddlers need to be able to follow instructions and understand why using the toilet is necessary
  7. Training should take place in a warm, relaxed, supportive manner
  8. Punishment or harsh discipline should not be used for toilet training

II. **Cognitive development**
  A. **Piaget's theory of cognitive development: Sensorimotor stage (birth - 2 years)** (Piaget, 1952)
    1. The sensorimotor stage is the first of Piaget's four stages of cognitive development
    2. During this stage, infants become progressively better able to organize and coordinate sensations with physical movements and actions.
    3. Infants acquire **object permanence**, the ability to understand that objects and events continue to exist even though the infant can no longer see or hear or touch them.
    4. The sensorimotor period is subdivided into six substages
      a. **Simple reflexes** (0 - 1 month)
        (1) In this substage, reflexive behaviors, such as rooting and sucking, are used
        (2) Infants begin to be able to produce behaviors that resemble reflexes even when the stimuli is only nearby
      b. **First habits and secondary circular reactions** (1 - 4 months)
        (1) In this substage, infants learn to coordinate sensations and actions
        (2) A **habit** is a scheme based upon a simple reflex, such as sucking, that is completely separate from its eliciting stimulus
        (3) A **primary circular reaction** involves repeating an action using the body, such as kicking
      c. **Secondary circular reactions** (4 - 8 months)
        (1) In this substage, infants become more object-oriented or focused on the world, moving beyond preoccupation with the self in sensorimotor interactions
        (2) **Secondary circular reactions** involve repeating actions with objects, for example, shaking a rattle
        (3) Infants imitate simple actions of others, such as physical gestures
      d. **Coordination of secondary circular reactions** (8 - 12 months)
        (1) Infants combine previously learned schemes
        (2) Actions become even more outwardly directed than before
        (3) Infants achieve intentionality
      e. **Tertiary circular reactions, novelty, and curiosity** (12 - 18 months)
        (1) Infants become intrigued by the variety of properties that objects possess and by the many things they can make happen to objects
        (2) **Tertiary circular reactions** are schemes in which the infant explores new possibilities with objects, continually changing what is done to them and exploring the results
        (3) Previous circular reactions focused on repeating former actions; infant first becomes interested in novel actions during this substage
      f. **Internalization of schemes** (18 - 24 months)
        (1) Infants' mental functioning shifts from sensorimotor to symbolic in nature, and they develop the ability to use primitive symbols
        (2) A **symbol** is an internalized sensory image or word that represents an event
    5. Some researchers have criticized Piaget's theory on the grounds that infants develop memory and symbolic activity earlier than Piaget thought -- he may have underestimated infants' abilities
  B. **Information processing perspective on infant cognition**
    1. Information processing theorists focus on cognitive processes such as attention, memory and thinking
    2. **Habituation:** Repeated presentation of the same stimulus causes reduced attention to the stimulus, that is, infants get "bored" and pay less attention to a stimulus after they've seen it for a while
    3. **Dishabituation:** An infant's renewed interest in a stimulus; if a stimulus is changed and the infant can detect that change, the infant becomes more attentive to the stimulus
    4. Habituation is indicative of an infant's maturity and well-being
    5. Infants who have brain damage do not habituate well and may have developmental problems later

6. **Memory**
   a. Involves retaining information over time
   b. Memory develops earlier in infancy than was previously thought
   c. Infants as young as 2 1/2 months of age are able to remember some information

C. **Language development**
   1. **1 month:** Makes small, throaty sounds; cries
   2. **2 to 3 months:** Cries less
   3. **3 to 4 months:** Coos, making vowel-like sounds
   4. **4 to 5 months:** Shows an interest in sounds, responds to voices
   5. **6 to 7 months:** Babbles with consonant sounds, polysyllabically
   6. **8 to 9 months:** Imitates and repeats sounds; understands some words; infants' receptive vocabularies (the words they understand) develop before their spoken vocabularies (the words they are able to produce); comprehension still limited
   7. **9 to 12 months:** Understands some instructions
   8. **10 to 15 months:** First word spoken; first words are **holophrases**, single words that are used to imply a complete sentence
   9. **15 months:** Uses 4 to 6 words, knows "no"
   10. **18 to 24 months:** **Telegraphic speech**, the use of short and precise words to communicate with two-word utterances; at 18 months knows 10 or more words; at 24 months has a spoken vocabulary of 200 to 300 words

D. **Developmental Assessment**
   1. **Apgar scale**
      a. Used to assess the health of newborns at 1 and 5 minutes after birth
      b. Evaluates infants' heart rate, respiratory effort, muscle tone, body color, and reflex irritability
      c. Newborns given a score or 0, 1, or 2 on each of the health signs
      d. A score of 7 to 10 indicates the newborn is in good condition
      e. A score of 5 to 7 indicates fair condition
      f. A score of 3 or below indicates poor condition
   2. **Brazelton Neonatal Behavioral Assessment Scale**
      a. Given several days after birth to assess the newborn's neurological development, reflexes, and reactions to people
      b. Examiner rates the newborn in 27 categories
   3. The **Gesell** developmental quotient is an overall developmental score that combines subscores in motor, language, adaptive, and personal-social domains in the Gesell assessment of infants
   4. **Bayley Scales of Infant Development**
      a. Widely used
      b. Three components
         (1) Mental scale
         (2) Motor scale
         (3) Infant behavior profile
   5. **Information processing tasks**
      a. Infant habituation and dishabituation tasks have recently been found to predict intelligence in childhood
      b. Infants who habituate faster to a familiar stimulus and who more readily dishabituate to a novel stimulus tend to have higher IQ scores later

III. **Socioemotional development**
   A. **Social**
      1. **1 month:** Watches faces when spoken to
      2. **2 to 3 months:** Smiles in response to person or object; laughs aloud
      3. **4 to 5 months:** Recognizes familiar person or object; enjoys social interaction
      4. **6 to 7 months:** Becomes attached to primary caregiver, stranger anxiety begins

5. **8 to 9 months:** Reaches for familiar people, pushes away from strangers, cries when scolded, responds to own name
6. **10 to 12 months:** May become attached to security blanket, enjoys familiar settings, fearful in strange settings, uses mother for security
7. **15 to 18 months:** Temper tantrums, ritualistic behaviors, peak of thumbsucking
8. **24 months:** Increasing independence, can help undress self and pull on simple clothes, does not share possessions ("mine")

B. **Infant-caregiver attachment**
1. **Attachment** is a close emotional bond between the infant and the caregiver(s)
2. The first year of life is critical for the development of attachment
3. By 6 to 7 months of age, attachment to the caregiver(s) becomes more intense and focused on the primary caregiver
4. Caregiver's sensitivity to the infant's signals increases secure attachment
5. Individual infants differ in how securely they are attached to their caregiver(s)
6. A **securely attached** infant uses the caregiver, usually the mother, as a secure base from which to explore the environment
7. An **insecurely attached** infant avoids the mother or is ambivalent to her
8. Many toddlers develop a strong attachment to a soft toy or a particular blanket; toddlers get comfort from security objects; will eventually abandon the security object as they become more sure of themselves

C. **Temperament**
1. An individual's behavioral style and characteristic way of responding
2. An important influence on socioemotional development
3. **Three basic types of temperament** (Chess & Thomas, 1977)
   a. **Easy child**
      (1) Generally in a positive mood
      (2) Quickly establishes regular routines in infancy
      (3) Adapts easily to new experiences
   b. **Difficult child**
      (1) Tends to react negatively and cry frequently
      (2) Engages in irregular daily routines
      (3) Slow to accept new experiences
   c. **Slow-to-warm-up child**
      (1) Low activity level
      (2) Somewhat negative
      (3) Shows low adaptability
      (4) Displays a low intensity of mood
4. **Three components of temperament** (Buss & Plomin, 1984)
   a. **Emotionality:** The tendency to be distressed
   b. **Sociability:** The tendency to prefer the company of others to being alone
   c. **Activity level:** Tempo and vigor of movement

D. **Emotional expressions** (Izard, 1982)
1. Interest, neonatal smile, startled response, distress, and disgust are present at birth
2. Social smile appears at about 4 to 6 weeks
3. Anger, surprise, and sadness are seen at about 3 to 4 months
4. Fear emerges at about 5 to 7 months
5. Shame and shyness appear at about 6 to 8 months
6. Contempt and guilt emerge at about 2 years of age

E. **Erikson's psychosocial stages** (Erikson, 1968)
  1. **Trust vs. mistrust (birth - 1 year)**
     a. Infants learn trust when they are cared for in a consistent, warm manner and when their basic needs are taken care of by responsive, sensitive caregivers
     b. If an infant is not well fed and kept warm and taken care of on a consistent basis, a sense of mistrust is likely to develop
  2. **Autonomy vs. shame and doubt (1 - 3 years)**
     a. At this age, infants begin to assert their sense of independence or autonomy and exhibit a definite will of their own
     b. Infants feel pride in their own accomplishments and want to do everything themselves
     c. If restrained too much or punished too harshly, they are likely to develop a sense of shame and doubt
     d. If caregivers are impatient and do things for the toddler that the toddler can do himself, toddlers may develop a sense of shame and doubt
F. **Freud's psychoanalytic theory** (Freud, 1917)
  1. **Personality structures**
     a. **Id:** Consists of instincts
     b. **Ego:** Deals with the demands of reality
     c. **Superego:** The moral branch of personality that takes into account whether something is right or wrong
  2. **Defense mechanisms** are the unconscious methods by which the ego distorts reality, thereby protecting it from anxiety
  3. **Repression** is the most powerful defense mechanism; it works to push unacceptable id impulses out of awareness and back into the unconscious mind
  4. **Psychosexual stages during infancy**: Two of Freud's five stages are experienced during infancy
     a. The **oral stage** occurs during the first 18 months of life, in which the infant's pleasure centers around the mouth
     b. The **anal stage** occurs between 1 1/2 and 3 years of age, and during this stage the child's greatest pleasure involves the anus or the eliminative functions associated with it
G. **Play/stimulation/toys**
  1. **General guidelines**
     a. Caregivers should play with infants, give them toys, and periodically provide them with undivided attention during the course of the day
     b. Caregivers should be sensitive to individual infant's stimulation needs; some infants can't handle high levels of stimulation and become overwhelmed and cry and fuss when there is too much stimulation; other infants like a lot of stimulation and can benefit from it
     c. Infant play is usually solitary or involves interacting with adult
     d. Toddlers engage in solitary play as well as **parallel play** which involves playing separately from others, but with toys like those the others are using or in a manner that mimics their play
  2. **Birth to 1 month**
     a. Look at infants within close range
     b. Hang, hold objects about 8 to 10 inches from the infants' faces
     c. Rock infants, place them in a cradle
     d. Provide visually attractive crib and walls near the crib
  3. **2 to 3 months**
     a. Provide brightly colored toys
     b. Take infants to different rooms while you do chores
     c. Cradle gyms
     d. Rocking cribs or cradles
     e. Turn on musical toys and place them where infants can see them
     f. Place objects in the infants' hands or within the infants' reach

g. Give infants only objects that are safe to go in the mouth
4. **4 to 6 months**
   a. Let infants look at themselves in mirrors
   b. Give infants brightly colored toys, such as rattles, that they can grasp
   c. Place toys near infants so they can be reached
   d. Bounce infants on lap while holding in a standing position
   e. Help infants roll over
   f. Initiate an action, wait for the infants to imitate it, then repeat the action
   g. Weighted or suction toys
5. **6 to 9 months**
   a. Give infants large toys with bright colors, movable parts, and noisemakers
   b. Mirror
   c. Peekaboo
   d. Make funny noises to encourage imitation
   e. Place toys out of reach and encourage infants to get them
   f. Play pat-a-cake
   g. Activity boxes for the crib
   h. Swings
   i. Balls
6. **9 to 12 months**
   a. Show infants large pictures in books
   b. Take infants to places where there are animals, many people, different objects
   c. Play ball by rolling ball to infants
   d. Demonstrate how to throw ball
   e. Demonstrate building a two-block tower
   f. Play hide-the-doll-under-the-blanket
7. **Other suggested toys for the first 12 months**
   a. Soft, stuffed toys
   b. Mobiles
   c. Simple musical toys
   d. Strings of big beads and large snap toys
   e. Squeeze toys
   f. Teething toys
   g. Books with textures
   h. Simple take-apart toys
   i. Push-pull toys
   j. Exercise crib toys
8. **12 to 24 months**
   a. Dolls
   b. Balls
   c. Water toys
   d. Manipulative toys such as shapes, blocks, cars
   e. Telephone
   f. Play furniture, dishes
   g. Straddle toys and rocking horse
   h. Clay, sandbox toys, crayons, finger paints
   i. Pounding toys
   j. Push-pull toys
   k. Blocks

H. **Parent/child issues**
  1. **Birth to 6 months**
     a. Adjusting to newborn, postpartal parental emotional needs
     b. Understanding infant's need for environmental stimulation
     c. Being aware of and sensitive to infants's individual needs and temperament
     d. Establishing a schedule that meets infant's and family's needs
     e. Encouraging infant's growing social responsivity
  2. **6 months to one year**
     a. Being aware of infant's strengthening attachment to caregiver(s) and avoiding long separations from them
     b. Understanding infant's increasing stranger anxiety
     c. Providing appropriate, safe environment for infant's increasing mobility
  3. **2 years**
     a. Adjusting to toddler's increasing autonomy and individuality
     b. Allowing for child's need for independence while consistently setting realistic limits for child
     c. Reinforcing desired behavior
     d. Punishing immediately after undesired behavior
     e. Realizing that sharing possessions will be difficult at this age
     f. Understanding that negativity is typical of this age
I. **Day care**
  1. Many parents are concerned about the effects of day care on children
  2. The number of young children in day care has been increasing
  3. Quality of care children receives varies greatly
  4. Parents should be careful about the quality of day care they select for infants, especially for those under 1 year of age
  5. Children in high quality day care do not appear to be at risk in any way
  6. Children in low quality day care are less likely to be socially competent in early childhood
  7. **National Association for the Education of Young Children's (1986) recommendations concerning quality day care**
     a. **The adult caregivers**
        (1) The adults should enjoy and understand how infants and young children grow
        (2) There should be enough adults to work with a group and to care for the individual needs of children -- more specifically, there should be no more than four infants for each adult caregiver, no more than eight 2- to 3-year-old children for each caregiver, and no more than ten 4- to 5-year-old children for each adult caregiver
        (3) Caregivers should observe and record each child's progress and development
     b. **The program activities and equipment**
        (1) The environment should foster the growth and development of young children working and playing together
        (2) A good center provides appropriate and sufficient equipment and play materials and makes them readily available
        (3) Infants and children should be helped to increase their language skills and to expand their understanding of the world
     c. **The relation of staff to families and the community**
        (1) A good program should consider and support the needs of the entire family
        (2) Parents should be welcome to observe, discuss policies, make suggestions, and work in the activities of the center
        (3) The staff in a good center should be aware of and contribute to community resources -- the staff should share information about community recreational and learning opportunities with families

d. **The facility and the program should be designed to meet the varied demands of infants and young children, their families, and the staff**
   (1) The health of children, staff, and parents should be protected and promoted -- the staff should be alert to the health of each child
   (2) The facility should be safe for children and adults
   (3) The environment should be spacious enough to accommodate a variety of activities and equipment -- more specifically, there should be a minimum of 35 square feet of usable playroom floor space indoors per child and 74 square feet of play space outdoors per child

J. **Child maltreatment**
   1. **Forms of maltreatment**
      a. **Physical abuse**
         (1) Involves physical injury to the child
         (2) Minor physical abuse more common than major physical abuse
      b. **Physical neglect**
         (1) Failure to provide adequate nourishment, shelter, clothing, or health care
         (2) Accounts for a large proportion of reported cases of child maltreatment
      c. **Emotional abuse**
         (1) Parental behaviors that cause emotional and psychological harm to the child but are not physical abuse or neglect
         (2) Immediate effects of emotional abuse are often invisible
         (3) Less likely to be reported
      d. **Sexual abuse**
         (1) Sexual behaviors are forced upon the child
         (2) Girls at higher risk than boys
   2. **Parental risk factors**
      a. History of abuse in their background
      b. Difficulty controlling aggressive impulses
      c. Low self-esteem, lack of identity
      d. Often young, immature, dependent
      e. Often expect child to provide them with love and nurturing
      f. Socially isolated
      g. Lack of support from outside resources
      h. Lack of knowledge about child rearing
      i. Unrealistic expectations of child's abilities
      j. Low tolerance for common infant behaviors
   3. **Child risk factors**
      a. Difficult temperament
      b. Special needs
      c. Premature
      d. Unattractive children
      e. Unwanted children
   4. **Cultural/environmental risk factors**
      a. Chronic stress
      b. Unemployment
      c. Alcohol or substance abuse
      d. Incidence of child abuse is higher in countries, such as the U.S., where there is much violence in the culture than in less violent cultures, such as China

5. **Signs of abuse**
   a. Many unexplained injuries, scars, bruises
   b. Inconsistent explanations for child's injuries
   c. Emotional response of parent inconsistent with the degree of the child's injury
   d. Physical signs of neglect such as malnourishment, dehydration, unkempt appearance
   e. Child cringes when approached and appears overly afraid
   f. Child has excessive interest in sexual matters
   g. Child has sexually transmitted disease
6. **Most states have mandatory reporting of abuse laws**

Infancy and Toddlerhood Review Questions

Rita and Raoul bring their one-month-old daughter, Marie, to the well-baby clinic. This is their first child, and they are concerned about Marie's development and how to best take care of her. They have been getting conflicting advice from various friends and family members.

Questions 1-9 refer to the above situation.

1. Rita's mother-in-law told her that babies are born blind. What can the nurse tell Rita about newborn vision?
   a. Babies are born with 20/20 vision just like adults.
   b. Babies are born with 20/100 vision, just a little worse than adults.
   c. Babies are born with visual acuity somewhere between 20/200 and 20/600.
   d. Babies are born totally blind.

2. Rita wants to put some pictures near Marie's crib but doesn't know what kind of pictures Marie would be most likely to prefer. What kinds of pictures do newborns prefer?
   a. bright pictures
   b. patterned pictures
   c. pastel pictures
   d. colorful pictures

3. Rita's sister has four children and they seem to thrive on the high levels of activity and noise at their home. However, every time Rita brings Marie to her sister's home, Marie cries. The fact that Marie cries a lot at her sister's highly stimulating home is likely to mean that
   a. Marie doesn't like Rita's sister.
   b. Marie is too young to be taken out of her own home.
   c. Marie is getting overstimulated.
   d. Marie prefers higher levels of stimulation.

4. Rita's sister has told her that she should provide Marie with more stimulation. Rita isn't sure how much stimulation is appropriate. The nurse should tell her that
   a. all babies need high levels of stimulation
   b. all babies need low levels of stimulation
   c. babies need more stimulation than older children
   d. babies vary in how much stimulation they need and she should be sensitive to Marie's signals to determine how much stimulation is appropriate

5. Raoul is concerned because Marie won't reach for toys or roll over. He is afraid that her development is delayed. At about what age should he expect Marie to be able to reach for objects and roll over?
   a. Marie should be able to now, at age one month.
   b. Marie should be able to at about 4 to 5 months of age.
   c. Marie should be able to at about 7 to 8 months of age.
   d. Marie should be able to at about 9 to 10 months of age.

6. Which of the following assessment procedures would most appropriately be used to determine whether Marie's development at one month is normal or delayed?
   a. Apgar scale
   b. Alpha-fetoprotein test
   c. Bayley Scales of Infant Development
   d. It is not possible to accurately assess development at that young of an age.

7. Raoul wants to know when Marie will be old enough so he can play with her. What kinds of suggestions might the nurse give him about activities he could do with Marie now? He could
   a. rock her and hold different toys up about 8 inches in front of her
   b. play pat-a-cake with her
   c. place toys out of reach and encourage Marie to get them
   d. give her manipulative toys such as blocks and cars

8. Raoul wants Rita to stop breast-feeding and use a bottle instead. Rita's friend has told her that all babies should be breastfed until they are two years old. What could the nurse tell Rita about the benefits of breast-feeding vs. bottle-feeding?
   a. There really isn't any substantial difference between the benefits of the two methods.
   b. Bottle-feeding provides the infant with better nutrition than breast-feeding.
   c. Breast-feeding gives the infant immunity from some diseases during the first few months of life.
   d. Bottled milk is more easily digested by infants.

9. Rita has noticed that whenever she touches the side of Marie's mouth, Marie turns her head and opens her mouth. She wonders if this is normal. The nurse can tell her that it is a normal infant reflex called the
   a. rooting reflex
   b. Moro reflex
   c. sucking reflex
   d. Babinski reflex

10. Maggie just gave birth to a premature baby. What can the nurse tell her about the developmental outcomes associated with premature birth?
   a. Socioeconomic status is unrelated to developmental outcomes.
   b. Premature infants are not considered high risk infants.
   c. The more premature babies weigh and the closer to term they are born, the less risk of negative outcomes.
   d. Premature babies with no visible problems are at equal risk as premature babies with visible problems.

11. At what age does the incidence of Sudden Infant Death Syndrome (SIDS) peak?
   a. 2 to 4 months
   b. 6 to 8 months
   c. 10 to 12 months
   d. 15 to 18 months

12. At birth, the average infant weighs _____ and is _____ in length.
   a. 3 pounds; 15 inches
   b. 5 pounds; 17 inches
   c. 7 1/2 pounds; 20 inches
   d. 10 1/2 pounds; 23 inches

13. By one year of age, infants have usually _____ their birthweight.
   a. doubled
   b. tripled
   c. quadrupled
   d. quintupled

14. The first teeth usually emerge at about
   a. 1 month
   b. 2 months
   c. 6 months
   d. 12 months

15. Motor development milestones
   a. do not vary by more than 1 month in normal infants
   b. occur in different sequences for different infants
   c. occur in the same sequence for most infants
   d. occur in different sequences for developmentally delayed and normal infants

16. By about 6 months of age, the average infant can
   a. walk using furniture for support
   b. crawl
   c. walk without assistance
   d. sit without support

17. The average infant first begins to walk without assistance at about
   a. 6 months
   b. 9 to 10 months
   c. 12 to 13 months
   d. 15 to 16 months

18. An average 2-month-old infant is able to
   a. hold a toy but will not reach for it
   b. reach for an object and bring it to her mouth
   c. transfer a toy from one hand to another
   d. use a pincer grasp

19. At birth, most infants
   a. are able to hear
   b. do not respond to touch
   c. show a preference for sour tastes
   d. are not able to distinguish between tastes

20. Solid foods are usually introduced when the baby is about
   a. 2 months of age
   b. 6 months of age
   c. 12 months of age
   d. 18 months of age

21. Lauren has a 1-year-old infant and is wondering when she should begin potty training. When should toilet training typically begin?
   a. 12 to 13 months
   b. 15 to 18 months
   c. 20 to 24 months
   d. 36 months

22. During the first month of life, thinking primarily involves
   a. reflexive behaviors
   b. habits
   c. imitating others
   d. intentional behaviors

23. According to Piaget, infants begin to use symbols in their thought at
    a. birth
    b. 6 months of age
    c. 12 months of age
    d. 18 to 24 months of age

24. Twelve-month-old Christian's language development is average. He is likely to
    a. be cooing
    b. be babbling
    c. have spoken his first word
    d. use telegraphic speech

25. Infants who habituate to stimuli more rapidly are predicted to have
    a. higher future intelligence
    b. lower future intelligence
    c. an attention deficit disorder
    d. future socioemotional difficulties

26. Newborn Kaneesha receives an Apgar score of 10. The nurse tells Kaneesha's mother that this score indicates that Kaneesha is in
    a. good condition
    b. fair condition
    c. poor condition
    d. critical condition

27. Baby Alex is likely to develop an intense attachment focused on his mother, who is his primary caregiver, at about
    a. 2 months
    b. 6 to 7 months
    c. 10 to 12 months
    d. 18 to 24 months

28. During the first year of her life, Rachel was cared for by her rather cold, unresponsive, and insensitive mother. Erikson would predict that Rachel will develop a sense of
    a. autonomy
    b. shame and doubt
    c. mistrust
    d. trust

29. According to Freud, during the first year of life infant's pleasure is focused on
    a. the anus
    b. the mouth
    c. the genitals
    d. the phallus

30. A parent who fails to provide adequate nourishment, shelter, clothing, or health care for a child has committed which form of child maltreatment?
    a. emotional abuse
    b. physical abuse
    c. physical neglect
    d. sexual abuse

Infancy and Toddlerhood Review Answers

1. c
2. b
3. c
4. d
5. b
6. c
7. a
8. c
9. a
10. c
11. a
12. c
13. b
14. c
15. c
16. d
17. c
18. a
19. a
20. b
21. c
22. a
23. d
24. c
25. a
26. a
27. b
28. c
29. b
30. c

SECTION IV   CHILDHOOD AND ADOLESCENCE CONCEPT REVIEW

Early Childhood Review (3 to 5 years)

I. **Physical development**
   A. **Height**
      1. During early childhood, the average child grows 2 1/2 inches per year
      2. The percentage of increase in height decreases each year
      3. From 2 to 6 years of age, girls are only slightly smaller than boys
      4. Height differences between children are due mainly to ethnic origin and nutrition
      5. Unusual shortness can be due to congenital factors, physical problems that develop during childhood, or emotional difficulties
         a. Congenital growth problems can sometimes be treated with hormones directed to the pituitary gland
         b. Malnutrition and chronic infections can stunt growth during early childhood
         c. **Deprivation dwarfism** is a type of growth retardation caused by emotional deprivation; children are deprived of affection which causes stress and alters the release of hormones by the pituitary gland
   B. **Weight**
      1. The average child gains between 5 and 7 pounds per year during early childhood
      2. The percentage of increase in weight decreases each year
      3. Girls are only slightly lighter than boys
      4. Children tend to slim down during the preschool years as their trunks lengthen
      5. Body fat steadily declines
      6. Girls have more fatty tissue than boys; boys have more muscle tissue than girls
   C. **The brain**
      1. The brain continues to grow during childhood but not as quickly as during infancy
      2. By 3 years of age, the brain is 3/4 of its adult size
      3. By 5 years of age, the brain is 9/10 of its adult size
      4. The brain and head grow more rapidly than other parts of the body
      5. **Myelination** is a process in which nerve cells are covered and insulated with a layer of fat cells; this process has the effect of increasing the speed of information traveling through the nervous system
      6. Myelination is related to the maturation of many abilities
      7. Myelination in areas of the brain related to eye-hand coordination is complete at about 4 years of age
   D. **Gross motor skills**
      1. **3 years**
         a. Hop
         b. Jump 6 inches
         c. Jump off a step
         d. Run back and forth
         e. Ride a tricycle
         f. Walk up stairs alternating feet
      2. **4 years**
         a. Become more adventurous in their running and jumping
         b. Go down stairs with just one foot on each step
         c. Skip
         d. Hop on one foot

3. **5 years**
   a. Become even more adventuresome
   b. Climb
   c. Run hard and race
   d. Can balance on one foot for about 10 seconds
   e. Jump rope
   f. Roller skate
4. **Throughout the preschool years, children are very, very active and need daily exercise**

E. **Fine motor skills**
   1. **3 years**
      a. Clumsily pick up tiny objects with thumb and forefinger
      b. Build high block towers and 3-block bridge
      c. Put together simple jigsaw puzzles and form boards
   2. **4 years**
      a. Fine motor coordination becomes more precise
      b. Button buttons and lace shoes
      c. Use scissors to cut outline
   3. **5 years**
      a. Further improvements in fine motor coordination
      b. Enjoy building houses or churches instead of simple towers
      c. Draw a picture of a person
      d. May tie shoelaces

F. **Handedness**
   1. Hand preference is usually noticed during early childhood but can be present during infancy
   2. Some preschool children continue to use both hands throughout the preschool years with a definite hand preference not developing until later
   3. By 2 years of age, about 10 percent of children prefer using their left hand

G. **Nutrition**
   1. Individual energy requirements vary depending on activity level and **basal metabolism rate**, that is, the minimum amount of energy a person uses in a resting state
   2. Energy needs increase throughout the preschool years
   3. The average preschool child requires 1700 calories per day
   4. Except in cases of extreme obesity, overweight preschool children are not generally encouraged to lose weight but, rather, to slow their weight gain

H. **Illness and health**
   1. Dehydration and malnutrition as a result of diarrhea is the leading cause of childhood death in the world
   2. Many of the deaths caused by diarrhea could be prevented by **oral rehydration therapy** which is a treatment that involves a range of techniques designed to prevent dehydration during episodes of diarrhea by giving the child fluids by mouth
   3. Other disorders likely to be fatal during childhood include birth defects, cancer, and heart disease

I. **Accidents**
   1. Leading cause of death in U.S. for children over 1 year of age
   2. Automobile accidents and fire account for more than half of all child accidental deaths
   3. **Common types of accidents:** Many are due to children's curiosity and interest in exploring their environment; prevention through parent education and child protection is often possible
      a. **Motor vehicle**
         (1) Struck by vehicle while walking or running in the street, often chasing after objects thrown into the street
         (2) Children's small size makes it difficult to see them when backing out of a driveway
         (3) Improper use of restraining devices while riding in a car

34

   b. **Burns**
    (1) Pulling pan off the stove, playing with matches, inserting object into wall socket
    (2) Climbing onto stove, ironing board, to get cigarettes
   c. **Poisons**
   d. **Drowning**
   e. **Aspirating small objects and putting foreign bodies in ear or nose**
   f. **Fractures**

II. **Cognitive development**
 A. **Piaget's theory of cognitive development: Preoperational thought stage (2-7 years)** (Piaget, 1952)
  1. In general, thought is illogical and not well organized
  2. Children do not yet think in an operational way; **operations** are internalized sets of actions that allow children child to do mentally what was done physically before
  3. Children in this stage are just beginning to be able to think about what they have previously done physically
  4. Involves a transition from primitive to more sophisticated use of symbols
  5. **Two substages of the preoperational thought stage**
   a. **Symbolic function substage (2-4 years)**
    (1) In this substage, children gain the ability to mentally represent an object that is not present
    (2) Children make scribbles to represent people, houses, cars, clouds, etc.
    (3) During preschool years, drawings are fanciful and inventive, not realistic; they'll become more realistic, precise, and neat during the elementary school years
    (4) **Egocentrism** is a salient feature of preoperational thought; it is the inability to distinguish ones own perspective from someone else's perspective
    (5) **Animism** is common in preoperational thought; it is the belief that inanimate objects have "lifelike" qualities and are capable of action
   b. **Intuitive thought substage (4-7 years)**
    (1) In this substage, children begin to use primitive reasoning and want to know the answers to all sorts of questions
    (2) Thinking is intuitive rather than logical
    (3) Children have difficulty putting things into correct categories, classifications
    (4) **Centration** is a characteristic of thinking during this period; centration is the focusing, or centering, of attention on one characteristic to the exclusion of all others
    (5) Children in this stage lack **conservation**, a belief in the permanence of certain attributes of objects or situations in spite of superficial changes; for example, the understanding that a certain amount of liquid stays the same regardless of a container's shape
    (6) At this age, children ask a lot of questions because they are interested in reasoning and figuring out why things are the way they are
 B. **Information processing**
  1. **Attention**
   a. Improves significantly during the preschool years
   b. Toddlers spend little time focused on any one object or event
   c. Preschoolers might watch television for a half-hour
   d. Preschoolers generally have a deficit in **selective attention**, that is, they attend to the salient rather than the relevant features of a task
  2. **Memory**
   a. Short-term memory increases during early childhood
   b. At 2 to 3 years of age, children can remember about 2 digits in a memory span task
   c. By 7 years, they can remember about 5 digits

C. **Zone of proximal development (ZPD)**
   1. Vygotsky's term for tasks too difficult for children to master alone, but that can be mastered with the guidance and assistance of adults or more skilled children
   2. The lower limit of the ZPD is the level of performance children can reach working by themselves
   3. The upper limit of the ZPD is the level children can reach with assistance from an instructor
   4. ZPD is a measure of learning potential
   5. When attempting difficult tasks, children initially need teacher's help
   6. Goal is for children to gradually learn to perform at the same level without assistance
D. **Education**
   1. **Child-centered education**
      a. Involves the whole child
      b. Includes concern for the child's physical, cognitive and social development
      c. Instruction is organized around the child's needs, interests, and learning styles
      d. The process of learning, rather than what is learned, is emphasized
   2. **Developmentally-appropriate schooling is recommended**
      a. **Age appropriateness:** Schooling which is based upon knowledge of the typical development of children within an age span
      b. **Individual appropriateness:** Schooling which is based upon the uniqueness of the child
      c. This approach stresses a concrete, hands-on approach to learning
      d. Direct teaching largely through abstract, paper-and-pencil activities presented to large groups of young children is believed to be developmentally inappropriate
   3. **Education for disadvantaged children**
      a. **Project Head Start:** A compensatory preschool education program designed to provide children from low-income families the opportunity to acquire the skills and experiences important for success in school
      b. **Project Follow Through:** An adjunct to Project Head start devised to determine which programs were the most effective; enriched programs were continued through the first few years of elementary school
      c. **Factors associated with successful programs** (Schorr, 1989)
         (1) Successful programs are comprehensive and intensive
         (2) In successful programs, staff have the time, training, and skills that are needed to build relationships of trust and respect with children and families
         (3) Successful programs deal with the child as part of the family, and the family as part of the neighborhood and community
         (4) Successful programs cross long-standing professional and bureaucratic boundaries
E. **Language development** (Brown, 1973)
   1. **12 to 26 months**
      a. Vocabulary consists mainly of nouns and verbs, with some adjectives and adverbs
      b. Typical sentences: "Mommy bye-bye." "Big doggie."
   2. **27 to 30 months**
      a. Plurals are correctly formed, past tense is used, definite (*the*) and indefinite (*a*) articles are used, and some prepositions
      b. Typical sentences: "Dolly in bed." "Them pretty." "Milk's all gone."
   3. **31 to 34 months**
      a. Yes-no questions appear, *wh*-questions (*who, what, where*) common, negatives (*no, not, non*) are used, commands or requests are used
      b. Typical sentences: "Daddy come home?" "Susie no want milk."
   4. **35 to 40 months**
      a. One sentence is sometimes embedded in another
      b. Typical sentences: "I think it's red." "Know what I saw."

5. **41 to 46 months**
    a. Simple sentences and propositional relations are coordinated
    b. Typical sentences: "I went to Bob's and had ice cream." "I like bunnies 'cause they're cute."
6. During the preschool years, children become increasingly better at applying the rules of language
7. **Vocabulary**
    a. **3 years:** Vocabulary of about 300 words; 3- to 4-word sentences; some hesitation in speech patterns
    b. **4 years:** Vocabulary is about 1500 words or more
    c. **5 years:** Vocabulary is about 2100 words or more

III. **Socioemotional development**
  A. **Social development**
    1. **3 years**
        a. Begin to take turns
        b. Share
    2. **4 years**
        a. May have imaginary companion
        b. May be selfish, impatient
        c. Take pride in accomplishments
        d. Exaggerate, boast
        e. Tattle on others
    3. **5 years**
        a. Talk constantly
        b. Generally cooperative and sympathetic towards others
  B. **Erikson's third psychosocial stage: Initiative vs. guilt (preschool years)** (Erikson, 1968)
    1. Preschool children are challenged more than they were as infants
    2. To meet these challenges, they need to display active, purposeful behavior such as taking care of their bodies, their toys, and their pets
    3. Developing a sense of responsibility increases initiative
    4. If the child is irresponsible and feels anxious, uncomfortable guilt feelings may arise
  C. **Freud's third psychosexual stage** (Freud, 1917)
    1. **Phallic stage (3 to 6 years)**
    2. During this stage, pleasure focuses on the genitals as children discover that self-manipulation is enjoyable
    3. Identification with the same sex parent takes place
  D. **Play**
    1. **Parten's play categories** (Parten, 1932)
        a. **Unoccupied play**
            (1) Occurs when the child is not engaging in play as it is commonly understood and may stand in one spot, look around the room, or perform random movements that do not seem to have a goal
            (2) In the preschool years, unoccupied play is less frequent than other forms of play
        b. **Solitary play**
            (1) Child plays alone and independently of others
            (2) 2- to 3-year-olds engage more frequently in solitary play than older preschoolers do
        c. **Onlooker play**
            (1) Child watches other children play
            (2) May talk with other children and ask questions but does not enter into their play behavior

      d.   **Parallel play**
- (1) Child plays separately from others, but with toys like those the others are using or in a manner that mimics their play
- (2) Toddlers engage in this type of play more frequently than older preschoolers but even older preschoolers engage in parallel play quite often

      e.   **Associative play**
- (1) Play involves social interaction with little or no organization
- (2) Children seem to be more interested in each other than in the tasks they are performing
- (3) Borrowing or lending toys and following or leading one another in line are examples of associative play
- (4) Social play increases dramatically during the preschool years

      f.   **Cooperative play**
- (1) Involves social interaction in a group with a sense of group identity and organized activity
- (2) Children's formal games, competition aimed at winning, and groups formed by the teacher for doing things together are examples of cooperative play
- (3) Cooperative play is typical of the games of middle childhood

2. **Other types of play**

      a.   **Sensorimotor play**
- (1) Behavior engaged in by infants to derive pleasure from exercising their existing sensorimotor schemes
- (2) Begins at 4-6 months of age, decreases during preschool years

      b.   **Practice play**
- (1) Involves the repetition of behavior when new skills are being learned or when physical or mental mastery and coordination of skills are required for sports or games
- (2) Can be engaged in throughout life

      c.   **Pretense/symbolic play**
- (1) Occurs when the child transforms the physical environment into a symbol
- (2) Appears at about 18 months of age, reaches a peak at 4 to 5 years, then gradually declines

      d.   **Social play**
- (1) Involves social interaction with peers
- (2) Increases dramatically during the preschool years

      e.   **Constructive play**
- (1) Combines sensorimotor/practice repetitive activity with symbolic representation of ideas
- (2) Occurs when children engage in self-regulated creation or construction of a product or a problem solution
- (3) Increases in the preschool years as symbolic play increases and sensorimotor play decreases

3. **Games**

      a.   Activities engaged in for pleasure that include rules and often competition with one or more individuals

      b.   Preschoolers begin to participate in social game play that involves simple rules of reciprocity and turntaking

      c.   Games not as important to preschoolers as they are to elementary school children

4. **Toys**

      a.   Manipulative toys

      b.   Creative toys

      c.   Educational toys such as counting equipment, geometric puzzles

      d.   Construction sets

      e.   Musical toys

      f.   Large, simple puzzles

g. Form boards

h. Blocks

i. Painting, cutting tools

j. Toys that encourage imaginary play such as dress-up clothes, dolls, house, furniture, small trucks, animals

k. Playground equipment such as swings, slides, tricycles

E. **Gender**

1. **About gender**

   a. **Gender** refers to the social dimension of being male or female

   b. **Gender identity** is the sense of being male or female, which most children acquire by the time they are 3 years old

   c. **Gender role** is a set of expectations that prescribe how females and males should think, act and feel

2. **Biological influences**

   a. **Hormones** begin influencing male and female physical development prenatally

   b. **Androgen** is the main class of male sex hormones

   c. **Estrogen** is the main class of female sex hormones

   d. Children's behavior as males or females is due to an interaction of biological and environmental factors

3. **Social influences**

   a. Parents

   b. Culture

   c. Schools

   d. Peers

   e. Media

   f. Other family members

4. **Gender Theories**

   a. **Identification theory**

      (1) Based on Freud's view that the preschool child develops a sexual attraction to the opposite-sex parent, then by approximately 5 or 6 years of age renounces this attraction because of anxious feelings, and subsequently identifies with the same-sex parent, unconsciously adopting the same-sex parent's characteristics

      (2) No longer a popular theory

      (3) Contradicted by findings that children become gender-typed earlier than 5 or 6 years of age and even when the same-sex parent is not present in the family

   b. **Social learning theory of gender**

      (1) Emphasizes that children's gender development occurs through observation and imitation of gender behavior, and through the rewards and punishments children experience for gender appropriate and inappropriate behavior

      (2) Critics argue that gender development is not as passively acquired as this theory indicates

   c. **Cognitive developmental theory**

      (1) Children's gender typing occurs after they have developed a concept of gender

      (2) Once they consistently conceive of themselves as male or female, children often organize their world on the basis of gender

   d. **Gender schema theory**

      (1) A **schema** is a cognitive structure, a network of associations that organizes and guides an individual's perceptions

      (2) A **gender schema** organizes the world in terms of female and male

      (3) **Gender schema theory** states that an individual's attention and behavior are guided by an internal motivation to conform to gender-based sociocultural standards and stereotypes

39

F. **Moral development**
   1. Concerns rules and conventions about what people should do in their interactions with other people
   2. **Three domains of moral development**
      a. Reasoning or thinking about moral conduct
      b. Behavior in moral circumstances
      c. Feelings about moral matters
   3. **Piaget's view of the development of moral reasoning** (Piaget, 1932)
      a. **Heteronomous morality**
         (1) Occurs from 4 to 7 years of age
         (2) Justice and rules are conceived of as unchangeable properties of the world, removed from the control of people
         (3) Rightness or goodness of behavior determined by the consequences of the behavior, not the intentions of the actor
      b. **Autonomous morality**
         (1) About 10 years and older
         (2) Child becomes aware that rules and laws are created by people and that, in judging an action, one should consider the actor's intentions as well as the consequences
         (3) Children 7 to 10 years of age are in a transition between the two stages
   4. **Moral behavior**
      a. Processes of reinforcement, punishment, and imitation are used to explain children's moral behavior
      b. Moral behavior is influenced extensively by the situation
      c. Ability to resist temptation is closely tied to the development of self-control and the ability to delay gratification
      d. Cognitive factors are important in the child's development of self-control
   5. **Moral feelings**
      a. **Empathy** is reacting to another's feelings with an emotional response that is similar to the other's feelings
      b. **Positive feelings** such as empathy, sympathy, admiration, and self-esteem, as well as **negative feelings** such as anger, outrage, shame, and guilt, contribute to children's moral development
      c. These emotions influence children to act in accord with standards of right and wrong
G. **Parenting styles** (Baumrind, 1971, Maccoby & Martin, 1983)
   1. **Authoritarian**
      a. A restrictive, punitive style in which the child is told to follow the parent's directions and to respect work and effort
      b. Parent places firm limits and controls on the child with little verbal exchange allowed
      c. Associated with children's social incompetence, specifically, anxiety about social comparison, a lack of initiative, and poor communication skills
   2. **Authoritative**
      a. Encourages children to be independent but still places limits and controls on their actions
      b. Extensive verbal give-and-take is allowed
      c. Parents are warm and nurturant toward the child
      d. Associated with children's social competence
   3. **Permissive-indifferent**
      a. Parent is very uninvolved in the child's life
      b. Associated with children's social incompetence, especially a lack of self-control
   4. **Permissive-indulgent**
      a. Parents are highly involved with their children but place few demands or controls on them
      b. Associated with children's social incompetence, especially a lack of self-control

H. **Adapting parenting to changing developmental needs**
1. At 2 to 3 years, parents often use physical manipulation to handle disciplinary needs; for example, carrying them away from an undesirable activity, putting fragile and dangerous objects out of reach
2. As children get older, parents more often use reasoning, moral exhortation, and giving or withholding special privileges

I. **Parent-child issues**
1. Modesty
2. Bedtime rituals/word rituals
3. Control of temper
4. Fighting with siblings and peers
5. Eating behavior and manners
6. Autonomy in dressing
7. Attention seeking

J. **Effects of divorce on children**
1. Children experience considerable stress when their parents divorce and are at risk for developing problem behaviors
2. Age and sex of children may influence their adjustment to the divorce
3. Amount of conflict related to adjustment; children in divorced families low in conflict function better than children in intact, never-divorced homes high in conflict
4. Most children emerge from divorce as competent individuals
5. Developmentalists have been moving away from the view that single-parent families are atypical or pathological, focusing more on the diversity of children's responses to divorce and the factors that facilitate or disrupt children's development and adjustment

Middle Childhood Review (6 to 11 years)

I. **Physical development**
A. Growth is slow and consistent
B. **Height**
1. Children grow an average of 2 to 3 inches a year
2. At age 11, the average girl is 4 feet, 10 inches tall
3. At age 11, the average boy is 4 feet, 9 1/2 inches tall
4. Legs become longer and trunks become slimmer
C. **Weight**
1. Children gain about 5 to 7 pounds a year
2. Weight gain is due mainly to increases in skeletal and muscular systems
3. Muscle mass and strength increase
4. Boys are usually stronger than girls
5. "Baby" fat decreases
D. **Gross motor skills**
1. Motor development becomes smoother and more coordinated than it was in early childhood
2. Physical skills such as running, climbing, skipping rope, swimming, bicycle riding, and skating are mastered
3. Most children enjoy using these physical skills
4. Boys usually outperform girls in gross motor skills involving large muscle activity
5. Can sit and attend for longer periods of time but still need to be active
6. Physical activity is important for refining skills
7. Should be engaged in active, rather than passive, activities

E. **Fine motor skills**
   1. Continue to improve fine motor skills
   2. Girls usually outperform boys in fine motor skills
   3. **6 years**
      a. Hammer
      b. Paste
      c. Tie shoes
      d. Fasten clothes
   4. **7 years**
      a. Hands become steadier
      b. Prefer a pencil to a crayon for writing
      c. Printing becomes smaller
      d. Reverse fewer letters
   5. **8 to 10 years**
      a. Hands can be used more independently, easily, and precisely
      b. Write rather than print words
      c. Letter size becomes smaller and more even
   6. **10 to 12 years**
      a. Begin showing manipulative skills similar to those of adults
      b. Can produce the complex, intricate, and rapid movements needed to play musical instruments and produce high-quality crafts
F. **Health and illness**
   1. **Accident prevention** is still important at this age
      a. Bicycle safety (helmets)
      b. Skateboard safety
      c. Safety in competitive sports such as baseball, football, and soccer
   2. **Communicable diseases** should be prevented by following appropriate immunization schedules, proper rest and diet, and frequent medical and dental check-ups
   3. Sex education should begin at this age level
   4. Promotion of a balanced diet is important; high-calorie, low-nutrition snacks are popular and can lead to weight gain

II. **Cognitive development**
A. **Piaget's theory of cognitive development: Concrete operational thought stage (7-11 years)** (Piaget, 1952)
   1. Children have many competencies that were lacking in preschool years
   2. **Logical reasoning** replaces intuitive reasoning, but only in concrete circumstances
   3. Thinking is not yet abstract (can't imagine steps in algebraic equation, for example)
   4. Children are able to do mentally what they could do only physically before
   5. Can use **operations, mentally reversing actions**
   6. Can now **decenter**, that is, they consider several characteristics of an object rather than focusing on a single property of an object
   7. Now have **conservation** skills, that is, they understand the permanence of certain attributes of objects or situations in spite of superficial changes
   8. Can **classify** or divide things into different sets and subsets and consider interrelationships
B. **Information processing**
   1. Long-term memory increases during middle childhood
   2. Children use more strategies, such as rehearsal and imagery, when trying to remember something
   3. **Schemas**, cognitive structures consisting of a network of associations that organize and guide an individual's perceptions, influence the way children process information
   4. **Metacognition**, knowledge about the human mind and its workings that is accumulated through experience and stored in long-term memory, is beneficial in school learning

5. Children use **cognitive monitoring**, that is, they take stock of what they are currently doing, what they will do next, and how effectively the mental activity is unfolding

C. **Language development**
   1. Add more abstract words to their vocabulary
   2. By the end of the elementary school years, can usually apply many of the appropriate rules of grammar
   3. Reading becomes an important skill during elementary school years

D. **Intelligence**
   1. **Intelligence** is defined as verbal ability, problem-solving skills, and the ability to learn from and adapt to the experiences of everyday life
   2. **Mental age (MA)** is an individual's level of mental development relative to others
   3. **Intelligence quotient is the child's mental age divided by chronological age multiplied by 100 (IQ=MA/CA x 100)**
   4. Average IQ score is 100
   5. IQ scores follow a normal distribution, with most of the population falling in the middle range with fewer falling in the extremely high and low ranges
   6. **Intelligence tests**
      a. **Stanford-Binet**
         (1) One of the most widely used individual tests of children's intelligence
         (2) Given to persons from age 2 through adulthood
         (3) Includes verbal and nonverbal items
         (4) A general composite IQ score is obtained, reflecting overall intelligence
      b. **Wechsler Scales**
         (1) The other most widely used individual intelligence test
         (2) Separate versions for preschoolers, school-aged children, and adults
         (3) Yields overall IQ score, verbal IQ, performance IQ, and twelve subscale scores
   7. **Cultural bias**
      a. Early intelligence tests were culturally biased, favoring white, middle-class children
      b. Contemporary versions attempt to reduce cultural bias but are not completely successful
      c. Minority groups may encounter problems understanding the standard English language used in the questions
      d. **Culture fair tests** are designed to reduce cultural bias
         (1) May include items that are familiar to individuals from all socioeconomic and ethnic backgrounds
         (2) Or may have all the verbal items removed
         (3) Sometimes used as an alternative to standard intelligence tests, but a completely satisfactory alternative has not yet been found
   8. **Misuse of intelligence tests**
      a. Scores should be used with other information about the individual
      b. IQ scores can produce unfortunate stereotypes and expectations
      c. Intelligence or high IQ is not necessarily the ultimate human value

E. **Giftedness**
   1. People who are **gifted** have above average intelligence (an IQ of 120 or higher) and/or superior talent for something
   2. Previously, giftedness was thought to be associated with emotional distress
   3. Currently, it appears that gifted people tend to be more mature and have fewer emotional problems than others

F. **Mental retardation**
   1. A condition of limited mental ability in which the individual has a low IQ, usually below 70 on a traditional intelligence test, and has difficulty adapting to everyday life
   2. Mentally retarded individuals go through the same sequence of development as nonretarded individuals, but at a slower rate
   3. Expectations should be based on mental age not chronological age
   4. **Classifications of mental retardation**
      a. **Mild mental retardation**
         (1) The majority, about 89%, of mentally retarded individuals are in this classification
         (2) IQ's of 55 to 70
         (3) Can achieve a mental age of 8 to 12 years
         (4) Can learn to read, write, do arithmetic, achieve a vocational skill, and function in society
      b. **Moderate mental retardation**
         (1) About 6% are classified as moderately mentally retarded
         (2) IQ's of 40 to 54
         (3) Can achieve a mental age of 3 to 7 years
         (4) Can attain up to a second-grade level of skills
         (5) Can learn skills of daily living, social skills
         (6) May be able to support themselves as adults through some types of labor, sheltered workshop
      c. **Severe mental retardation**
         (1) About 3.5% of the mentally retarded are in the severe category
         (2) IQ's of 25 to 39
         (3) Learn to talk and engage in very simple tasks but require extensive supervision
      d. **Profound mental retardation**
         (1) Fewer than 1% of mentally retarded are in this category
         (2) IQ's below 25
         (3) Need constant supervision
   5. **Causes of mental retardation**
      a. **Organic retardation**
         (1) Mental retardation caused by a genetic disorder or by brain damage
         (2) Organic refers to the tissues or organs of the body, so there is some physical damage in organic retardation
         (3) Most individuals with organic retardation have IQ's between 0 and 50
      b. **Cultural-familial retardation**
         (1) A mental deficit in which no evidence of organic brain damage can be found
         (2) Individuals' IQ's range from 50 to 70
         (3) Mental deficits thought to result from the normal variation that distributes people along the range of intelligence scores above 50, combined with growing up in a below-average intellectual environment
G. **Learning disabilities (LD)**
   1. **Definition of a learning disability**
      a. Children with a learning disability are of normal intelligence or above
      b. Have difficulties in one or more academic areas but usually do not show deficits in other academic areas
      c. Are not suffering from some other conditions or disorders, such as sensory impairments, that could explain their learning problems
   2. May have problems with listening, thinking, memory, reading, writing, spelling, or math
   3. Estimates of the number of children with learning disabilities range from 1 percent to 30 percent

44

4. **Causes of learning disabilities**
   a. Relatively little is known
   b. Neurological impairment or brain damage is suspected in some cases
   c. Various diseases and infections, malnutrition, or other environmental or genetic factors might be involved
5. **Treatment**
   a. Learning disabilities are complex and multifaceted
   b. Need to identify the specific cognitive and academic deficits individual children have and tailor learning environments specifically to their needs

H. **Attention-Deficit Hyperactivity Disorder (ADHD)**
   1. A subtype of learning disability characterized by a short attention span, distractibility, and high levels of physical activity
   2. Estimates of the incidence of ADHD range from 1 percent to 5 percent of children
   3. Vast majority are identified in the first three grades of elementary school, when teachers notice they have difficulty paying attention, sitting still, and concentrating on their homework
   4. **Possible causes**
      a. Heredity
      b. Prenatal damage, caused by factors such as excessive drinking, using cocaine
      c. Diet
      d. Family dynamics
      e. Physical environment
   5. Approximately 4 times as many boys as girls are classified as having ADHD
   6. **Treatment**
      a. Family behavior counseling
      b. Drug therapy
         (1) Amphetamines, especially Ritalin, are most widely prescribed
         (2) About 20 percent of children treated with Ritalin do not respond to it
      c. Structuring the environment, social world

III. **Socioemotional development**
A. **Peers**
   1. Peers become increasingly more important as children spend more time with peers than they did during early childhood
   2. Friendships become more important
   3. Popularity with peers is a strong motivation for most children
   4. **Individual differences in popularity with peers**
      a. **Popular children**
         (1) Have good listening skills
         (2) Are effective communicators
         (3) Be themselves
         (4) Are happy
         (5) Show enthusiasm and concern for others
         (6) Are self-confident, but not conceited
      b. **Neglected children**
         (1) Receive little attention from their peers but are not necessarily disliked by their peers
         (2) To help neglected children interact more effectively with their peers
            (a) Help them attract attention from their peers in positive ways
            (b) Hold peers attention by asking questions, by listening in a warm and friendly ways, and by saying things about themselves that relate to the peers' interests
            (c) Teach them to enter groups more effectively

45

        c. **Rejected children**
            (1) Disliked by their peers
            (2) More likely to be disruptive and aggressive than are neglected children
            (3) More often have serious adjustment problems later in life than do neglected children .
            (4) To help rejected children interact more effectively with their peers
                (a) Help them to listen to peers and "hear what they say" instead of trying to dominate peer relations
                (b) Train them to join peers without trying to change what is taking place in the peer group

B. **Erikson's fourth psychosocial stage: Industry vs. inferiority (elementary school years)** (Erikson, 1968)
    1. Children become interested in how things are made and how they work
    2. When children are encouraged in their efforts to make and build and work (e.g. building a model airplane, fixing a bicycle, cooking), their sense of industry increases
    3. Parents who see their children's efforts at making things as "mischief" or "making a mess" encourage children's development of a sense of inferiority
    4. Social worlds beyond families, such as school, also contribute to a sense of industry or inferiority

C. **Freud's fourth psychosexual stage: Latency (6 years to puberty)** (Freud, 1917)
    1. The child represses all interest in sexuality and develops social and intellectual skills
    2. The activity channels much of the child's energy into emotionally safe areas and helps the child forget the highly stressful conflicts of the phallic stage

D. **Kohlberg's theory of moral development** (Kohlberg, 1976)
    1. Stresses that moral development is based primarily on moral reasoning and unfolds in stages
    2. Classifies children and adults in terms of their level of moral reasoning on the basis of the responses they give to hypothetical moral dilemmas
    3. **Level one: Preconventional reasoning**
        a. The lowest level in Kohlberg's theory of moral development
        b. Child shows no internalization of moral values -- moral reasoning is controlled by external rewards and punishment
        c. Before age 9, most children reason in a preconventional way
        d. **Two preconventional stages**
            (1) **Stage 1. Punishment and obedience orientation**
                (a) Moral thinking is based on punishment
                (b) Children obey because adults tell them to obey
            (2) **Stage 2. Individualism and purpose**
                (a) Moral thinking is based on rewards and self-interest
                (b) Children obey when they want to obey and it is in their best interest to obey
                (c) What is right is what feels good and what is rewarding

E. **The self**
    1. During middle and late childhood, self-understanding shifts from defining oneself through external characteristics to defining oneself through internal characteristics
    2. Increasing **social comparison**, thinking about what they can do in comparison to others, occurs
    3. **Self-esteem** is the global evaluative dimension of the self; also referred to as self-worth or self-image
    4. **Self-concept** refers to domain-specific evaluations of the self
    5. **Four key aspects of improving self-esteem** (Bednar, Well, & Peterson, 1989; Harter, 1990)
        a. **Identifying the causes of low self-esteem and which domains of competence are important to the self:** Children have the highest self-esteem when they perform competently in domains important to themselves
        b. **Emotional support and social approval:** Both adult and peer support are important influences

      c.   **Achievement:** Teaching skills often results in increased achievement and enhanced self-esteem

      d.   **Coping:** Facing a problem and coping with it rather than avoiding it enhances self-esteem

F. **Gender**

  1. **Gender-role stereotypes**

      a.   Broad categories that reflect our impressions and beliefs about females and males

      b.   Stereotypical gender beliefs increase during the preschool years, peak in the early elementary school years, and then decrease in the middle and late elementary school years

  2. **Gender similarities and differences**

      a.   In the past, a number of differences between females and males have been exaggerated

      b.   **Three factors to keep in mind when looking at gender differences**

          (1) The differences are average, not all females versus all males

          (2) Even when differences are reported, there is considerable overlap between the sexes

          (3) The differences may be due primarily to biological factors, sociocultural factors, or both

      c.   **Physical differences**

          (1) From conception on, females are less likely than males to die

          (2) Females are less likely than males to develop physical or mental disorders

          (3) Males tend to grow taller than females

          (4) Females tend to have a higher percentage of body fat than males

      d.   **Cognitive differences**

          (1) More cognitive similarities than differences between males and females

          (2) At the gifted level, the average gifted male outperforms the average gifted female in math

          (3) Females have been reported to have higher verbal scores but more recent research suggests the differences are disappearing

      e.   **Social differences**

          (1) Most males are more active and aggressive than most females

          (2) Female gender role fosters helping that is nurturant and caring, whereas the male gender role promotes helping that is chivalrous

  3. **Androgyny** refers to the presence of desirable masculine and feminine characteristics in the same individual

G. **Play**

  1. **Constructive play**, which involves the creation or construction of a product or a problem solution, is a frequent form of play in the elementary school years

  2. **Games** are very important in the lives of elementary school age children; they like games with rules

  3. The highest incidence of game playing occurs between 10 and 12 years of age

  4. Competitive, challenging games enjoyed

  5. Commonly play tag, hopscotch, contests, jump rope, climb trees

  6. **Organized activities and clubs** are important

  7. In the beginning of the school years, boys and girls play together, but they gradually tend to play more with same-sex playmates

  8. Develop "best friends"

H. **Toys/activities**

  1. **6-to 9-year-olds**

      a.   Housekeeping toys

      b.   Word and number games

      c.   Physically active games such as jump rope, climbing trees

      d.   Collections of items such as baseball, basketball cards

      e.   Bicycle riding

      f.   Magic tricks

2. **9- to 12-year-olds**
   a. Enjoys group, team activities
   b. Crafts, needlework, beads
   c. Model kits, collections, hobbies
   d. Archery, dart games, chess, jigsaw puzzles
   e. Sculpturing materials such as pottery clay
   f. Science toys, magic sets
   g. Computer games

I. **Parent-child relations**
   1. **Issues**
      a. Fighting with siblings and peers
      b. Reaction to discipline
      c. Whether children should be made to perform chores and if so, whether they should be paid for them
      d. How to help children learn to entertain themselves rather than relying on parents for everything
      e. How to monitor children's lives outside the family in school and peer settings
      f. School-related difficulties
   2. **Discipline**
      a. Cognitive development has matured sufficiently to make it possible for parents to use reasoning
      b. Parents of school-age children usually use less physical discipline than they do parents of preschool children
      c. More likely to use deprivation of privileges
      d. Appeals directed at the child's self-esteem
      e. Comments designed to increase the child's sense of guilt
      f. Statements indicating to children that they are responsible for their actions
   3. **Children spend less time with parents than they do during early childhood**

J. **Societal changes in families**
   1. Increasing numbers of children are growing up in divorced and working-mother families
   2. Far more elementary and secondary school children than infant or preschool children live in stepfamilies
   3. Entrance of a stepparent can cause disequilibrium and stress for children
   4. Adjustment to a stepparent is less difficult when it occurs before adolescence rather than during adolescence
   5. Authoritative environments are associated with positive outcomes in children from divorced or stepfamily homes
   6. Latchkey children, those who are at home after school without parents being there, are more vulnerable to problems such as getting into trouble, stealing, vandalizing, and abusing a sibling

Adolescence Review (12 to 18-21 years)

I. **Physical development**
   A. **Puberty** is a period of rapid skeletal and sexual maturation that occurs mainly in early adolescence
   B. The hormonal and body changes occur about 2 years earlier in females (10 1/2 years of age is the average age) than in males (12 1/2 years is the average age)
   C. **Increased hormonal production**
      1. **Testosterone** is a hormone associated with the development of genitals, an increase in height, and a voice change in boys
      2. **Estradiol** is a hormone associated with breast, uterine, and skeletal development in girls

D. **Female areas of body change**
1. Height spurt
2. Menarche (average age of first menstruation is 12 1/2 years)
3. Breast growth
4. Growth of pubic hair
E. **Male areas of body change**
1. Height spurt
2. Penile growth
3. Testes growth
4. Growth of pubic hair
F. **Leading causes of mortality**
1. Accidents are the leading cause of death during adolescence
2. Motor vehicle accidents cause the most fatalities
3. Homicide is the second leading cause of death
4. Suicide is the third leading cause of death

II. **Cognitive development**
A. **Piaget's theory of cognitive development: Formal operational thought stage (11 to 15 through adulthood)** (Piaget, 1952)
1. Formal operational thought is more abstract than it was in earlier years
2. No longer limited to actual concrete experience
3. Can think of make-believe situations, hypothetical possibilities, and abstract propositions and reason about them
4. Increased interest in thinking about thought itself
5. Idealistic thinking
6. Logical thinking
B. **Adolescent egocentric thought** (Elkind, 1978)
1. The **imaginary audience** refers to adolescents' beliefs that others are as preoccupied with them as they themselves are
2. The **personal fable** is the part of adolescent egocentrism that involves adolescents' sense of uniqueness that makes them feel that no one can understand how they really feel

III. **Socioemotional development**
A. **Peers**
1. The pressure to conform to peers is strong during adolescence, especially during the eighth and ninth grades
2. Strong allegiance to cliques, clubs, organizations, and teams
3. Most adolescents are involved in dating
4. Interested in school-related activities and sports
B. **Erikson's fifth stage of psychosexual development: Identity vs. identity confusion (adolescence)** (Erikson, 1968)
1. A time of being interested in finding out who one is, what one is all about, and where one is headed in life
2. Adolescents experiment with numerous roles and identities they draw from the surrounding culture
3. Adolescents who successfully cope with these conflicting identities during adolescence emerge with a new sense of self
4. Adolescents who do not successfully resolve this identity crisis are confused, suffering from identity confusion
5. Adolescents with identity confusion either withdraw, isolating themselves from peers and family or they may lose their identity in the crowd

C. **Marcia's four statuses of identity:** Based on whether an adolescent has gone through a **crisis** (a period of identity development during which the adolescent is choosing among meaningful alternatives) and made a **commitment** (the part of identity development in which adolescents show a personal investment in what they are going to do) (Marcia, 1991)
   1. **Identity diffusion:** Adolescents who have not yet experienced a crisis (that is, they have not yet explored meaningful alternatives) or made any commitments
   2. **Identity foreclosure:** Adolescents who have made a commitment but have not experienced a crisis
   3. **Identity foreclosure:** Adolescents who are in the midst of a crisis, but their commitments are either absent or only vaguely defined
   4. **Identity achievement:** Adolescents who have undergone a crisis and have made a commitment
D. **Ethnic aspects of identity**
   1. Most ethnic minority individuals consciously confront their ethnicity for the first time in adolescence
   2. Become aware of the evaluations of their ethnic group by the majority culture
   3. Lack of successful ethnic minority role models with whom to identity is sometimes a concern
   4. Contexts in which youth live influence their identity development
E. **Freud's fifth psychosexual stage: Genital (adolescence through adulthood)** (Freud, 1917)
   1. A time of sexual reawakening
   2. Source of sexual pleasure now from someone outside the family
   3. Individual becomes capable of mature love relationship and independent functioning
F. **Kohlberg's level two of moral reasoning: Conventional reasoning** (Kohlberg, 1976)
   1. By early adolescence, most individuals reason morally in a conventional way
   2. At this level, the individual's internalization is intermediate
   3. The person abides by certain standards (internal), but they are the standards of others (external), such as parents or the laws of society
   4. **Two stages at the conventional level**
      a. **Stage 3. Interpersonal norms**
         (1) The person values trust, caring, and loyalty to others as the basis of moral judgments
         (2) Children often adopt their parents' moral standards at this stage, seeking to be thought of by their parents as a "good girl" or a "good boy"
      b. **Stage 4. Social system morality:** Moral judgments are based on understanding the social order, law, justice, and duty
G. **Teenage sexuality**
   1. The number of teenage females having intercourse has increased over the last 50 years
   2. Historically, boys have been more likely to experience sexual intercourse at an earlier age than girls, and have not shown as pronounced of a rise in teenage sexual behavior as girls have
   3. The majority of males and females have had sexual intercourse by the age of 19, with males being likely to become sexually active slightly earlier than females
   4. Problems associated with teenage sexuality include unwanted teen pregnancy and sexually transmitted diseases
H. **Teenage pregnancy**
   1. Increased health risks for mother and child
   2. **Mothers**
      a. Physical development not yet complete
      b. Developmental tasks of adolescence for identity and autonomy not yet completed
      c. Often drop out of school, less likely to complete high school
   3. **Infants**
      a. More likely to be low birthweight
      b. More likely to have neurological problems
      c. More likely to have childhood illnesses
      d. More likely to have abnormal developmental conditions

4. **Recommendations for reducing the high rate of teen pregnancy**
   a. Teaching abstention
   b. Improving sex-education and family-planning information
   c. Providing greater access to contraception
   d. Broad community involvement and support

I. **Eating disorders**
   1. **Anorexia nervosa**
      a. An eating disorder that involves the relentless pursuit of thinness through starvation
      b. Affects primarily females during adolescence and early adulthood
      c. Most individuals with this disorder are white and from well-educated, middle- and upper-income families
      d. Have a distorted body image
      e. Sometimes have families that place high demands for achievement
      f. By limiting their food intake, they gain a sense of control
   2. **Bulimia**
      a. An eating disorder that involves a binge-and-purge sequence on a regular basis
      b. Primarily a female disorder and is prevalent among college women
      c. Whereas anorexics can control their eating, bulimics cannot
      d. Depression is common among bulimics

J. **Drug use and abuse**
   1. After a downward trend in the use of illicit drugs since the 1960s and 1970s, there has recently been an increase in the use of marijuana, stimulants, LSD, and inhalants
   2. Alcohol is the drug most widely used by adolescents in the U.S.
   3. Many adolescents use some kind of drug at some point, only some abuse drugs
   4. Parents, peers, and social support play important roles in preventing adolescent drug abuse
   5. **Developmental model of adolescent drug abuse** (Brook, Brook, Gordon, Whiteman & Cohen, 1990)
      a. In childhood years, children fail to receive nurturance from their parents and grow up in conflict-ridden families
      b. Children fail to internalize their parents' personality, attitudes, and behavior, and later carry this lack of parental ties into adolescence
      c. Adolescent characteristics, such as lack of a conventional orientation and inability to control emotions are expressed in affiliations with peers who take drugs, which, in turn, leads to drug use
      d. Positive relationships with parents and others are important in reducing adolescents' drug use

K. **Suicide**
   1. Beginning at about the age of 15, the rate of suicide begins to rise rapidly
   2. Suicide accounts for about 12 percent of the mortality in the adolescent and young adult age group
   3. Males are about three times as likely to commit suicide as females
   4. Females attempt suicide more often than males but tend to use passive methods, such as sleeping pills, which are less likely to produce death
   5. **Proximal or immediate factors related to suicide**
      a. Highly stressful circumstances
      b. Loss of a boyfriend or girlfriend
      c. Poor grades at school
      d. Unwanted pregnancy
      e. Drugs
   6. **Distal or earlier factors related to suicide**
      a. History of family instability
      b. Long-term unhappiness, depression
      c. Lack of affection and emotional support by family

        d.   High control by parents

        e.   Pressure for achievement by parents

        f.   Lack of supportive friendships

        g.   Previous suicide attempts

L. **Juvenile delinquency** (Dryfoos, 1990)

   1.   Refers to a broad range of behaviors, from socially unacceptable behavior to status offenses to criminal acts

   2.   **Predictors of juvenile delinquency**

        a.   Negative identity

        b.   Low degree of self-control

        c.   Early initiation of delinquency

        d.   Being a male

        e.   Low expectations for education and little commitment to education

        f.   Heavy peer influence

        g.   Low resistance to peer pressure

        h.   Failure of parents to adequately monitor their adolescents

        i.   Ineffective discipline by parents

        j.   Living in an urban, high-crime, mobile neighborhood

   3.   **Successful programs**

        a.   Do not focus on delinquency alone (include other components such as education)

        b.   Have multiple components

        c.   Begin early in the child's development

        d.   Often involve schools

        e.   Focus on institutions while also giving individualized attention to delinquents

        f.   Include maintenance facets

M.   **At-risk youth** (Dryfoos, 1990, 1993)

   1.   High-risk behaviors in adolescence often overlap with four areas of special concern

        a.   Delinquency

        b.   Substance abuse

        c.   Adolescent pregnancy

        d.   School-related problems

   2.   Two approaches have the widest application to improving the lives of at-risk youth

        a.   Providing individual attention to at-risk children and adolescents

        b.   Developing broad community-wide interventions

N. **Ethnicity**

   1.   Much research on ethnic minority adolescents has not teased apart the influences of ethnicity and social class

   2.   Ethnicity and social class can interact and exaggerate the influence of ethnicity because ethnic minority individuals are overrepresented in the lower socioeconomic levels of U.S. society

   3.   Ethnic explanations of adolescent development have been given when socioeconomic explanations were more appropriate

   4.   Recognizing and respecting legitimate differences between various ethnic minority groups and between ethnic minority groups and the majority European-American group is an important aspect of getting along with others in a diverse, multicultural world

   5.   Ethnic minority groups are not homogeneous; they have different social, historical, and economic backgrounds

   6.   Value conflicts between **assimilation** (the absorption of ethnic minority groups into the dominant group, which often means the loss of some of the behavior and values of the ethnic minority group) and **pluralism** (the coexistence of distinct ethnic and cultural groups in the same society -- cultural differences are maintained and appreciated) can occur

O. **Parent-adolescent issues**
1. Adolescents push for autonomy and responsibility which may lead to conflict with parents
2. Parents need to relinquish control in those areas where the adolescent can make reasonable decisions but continue to guide the adolescent to make reasonable decisions in areas where the adolescent's knowledge is more limited
3. Conflict with parents escalates during early adolescence, remains somewhat stable during the high school years, and then lessens as the adolescent reaches 17 to 20 years of age
4. Conflict with parents can help the adolescent make the transition from being dependent on parents to becoming an autonomous individual
5. Most adolescents want to be treated like adults by 15 or 16 years of age

Childhood and Adolescence Review Questions

Due to the unexpected accidental death of her parents, 20-year-old Jennifer has suddenly assumed guardianship of her 4-year-old sister, Sara. She has found herself overwhelmed by her lack of understanding of 4-year-olds and how to raise them. She has turned to the nurse at the well-child clinic for assistance.

Questions 1-7 are based on the situation above.

1. Jennifer is concerned about Sara's reaction to her parents' deaths. What can the nurse tell Jennifer about the way that 4-year-olds typically think that might help her understand Sara's thoughts about her parents' dying?
   a. Preschoolers' thinking tends to be egocentric, therefore, Sara might blame herself for her parents' deaths.
   b. Preschoolers' thinking tend to be based on integrating senses and motor activities, therefore, Sara is likely to express her grief through motor activity.
   c. Preschoolers are able to decenter, therefore, Sara is likely to think about several different aspects of her parents' death at the same time.
   d. Preschoolers are able to think abstractly, therefore, so Sara is likely to ponder the meaning of death.

2. Jennifer is concerned because Sara won't sit still for an hour. What can the nurse tell Jennifer about normal motor development in 4-year-olds?
   a. Jennifer should be concerned because most 4-year-olds do like to sit still and play quietly for extended periods of time.
   b. Most 4-year-olds are extremely active, so Sara's high level of activity is probably normal.
   c. Girls usually are more active than boys, so Sara's restlessness is normal.
   d. Sara will probably not be able to sit still for extended periods of time until adolescence.

3. Which of the following parenting styles would be most likely to enhance Sara's socioemotional development?
   a. permissive-indifferent
   b. permissive-indulgent
   c. authoritative
   d. authoritarian

4. At four years of age, Sara is facing Erikson's developmental issue of
   a. trust vs. mistrust
   b. initiative vs. guilt
   c. industry vs. inferiority
   d. autonomy vs. shame and doubt

5. Jennifer remembers her parents using physical barriers and restraints to control Sara when she was younger. She's not sure whether she should continue to use this approach as Sara is getting older. What can the nurse tell Jennifer about changing discipline needs with age?
   a. A physical approach to discipline is the most effective method throughout childhood.
   b. As Sara gets older, more effective methods of discipline would be reasoning and withholding or granting privileges.
   c. As Sara gets older, she will not need to be disciplined.
   d. Caregivers should place few demands on children.

6. In which of the following types of play is Sara most likely to engage?
   a. make-believe
   b. solitary
   c. parallel
   d. game-playing

7. Which kind of toys or activities would be most appropriate for Sara?
   a. crafts
   b. push-pull toys
   c. model kits
   d. simple puzzles

8. Growth during early childhood is marked by
   a. continuing increases in the percentage of increase in height and weight each year
   b. an increase in body fat
   c. slimming down as trunks lengthen
   d. boys being significantly larger than girls

9. Myelination
   a. is complete at birth
   b. is related to the maturation of many abilities
   c. is not complete in areas related to fine motor coordination until adolescence
   d. decreases the speed of information traveling through the nervous system

10. The leading cause of childhood death in the world is
    a. cancer
    b. birth defects
    c. dehydration and malnutrition as a result of diahrrea
    d. heart disease

11. According to Piaget, preschool children are in the _____ stage of cognitive development.
    a. formal operational thought
    b. concrete operational thought
    c. sensory-motor
    d. preoperational thought

12. One characteristic of preoperational thought is
    a. conservation
    b. decentering
    c. reversibility
    d. animism

13. A 3-year-old is able to remember about _____ digits in a memory span task.
    a. 1
    b. 2
    c. 3
    d. 4

14. Education during the preschool years should
    a. involve using many paper-and-pencil activities
    b. be conducted in large groups
    c. be based on knowledge of the typical development of children of a particular age
    d. not be adjusted for individual variations in development

15. Growth during middle childhood
    a. is more rapid than during early childhood
    b. is slow and consistent
    c. occurs at the same rate as it did during infancy and early childhood
    d. is concentrated on the head and brain

16. Children 7 to 11 years of age are in Piaget's _____ stage of cognitive development
    a. sensory-motor
    b. concrete operational thought
    c. formal operational thought
    d. preoperational thought

17. Jerry is mildly mentally handicapped. At maturity, he would be expected to
    a. need constant supervision
    b. learn to talk and engage in only very simple tasks
    c. be able to work in a sheltered workshop
    d. learn to read, write, and learn a vocation

18. Katie has an IQ of 60, has no known brain damage or genetic disorder, and grew up in an unstimulating home environment. She appears to be
    a. within the normal range of intellectual development
    b. learning disabled
    c. culturally-familially retarded
    d. organically retarded

19. Which of the following could accurately describe a child with a learning disability?
    a. normal intelligence, difficulty in spelling but not math
    b. normal intelligence, visual impairment, having difficulty in reading
    c. mentally retarded, having difficulty in all academic areas
    d. above average intelligence, hearing impairment, having difficulty in all academic areas

20. Ten-year-old Jared has a short attention span, is very distractible, and has high levels of physical activity. Jared's behavior is characteristic of
    a. normal 10-year-old development
    b. ADHD
    c. mild mental retardation
    d. moderate mental retardation

21. Nine-year-old Lucinda loves to do craft projects. Her parents provide the materials she needs and praise her efforts. Lucinda is likely to develop a sense of
    a. autonomy
    b. trust
    c. identity
    d. industry

22. Nine-year-old Jeremiah likes to assemble model cars and try to repair things that are broken. His parents dislike the messes he makes when he does these things and discourage his efforts to make and repair things. Jeremiah is likely to develop a sense of
    a. mistrust
    b. identity confusion
    c. inferiority
    d. guilt

23. Which of the following toys or activities would be most appropriate to provide for a 10-year-old who is about to be hospitalized?
    a. games
    b. blocks
    c. manipulative toys
    d. balls

24. Adolescence is marked by
    a. a slowdown in growth
    b. steady growth
    c. rapid growth and sexual maturation
    d. decreased hormonal production

25. Anorexia nervosa
    a. is characterized by bingeing and purging
    b. is common in families with low demands for achievement
    c. is found more often in lower class than in middle and upper class families
    d. affects mostly females

26. Adolescent thought is generally
    a. abstract
    b. intuitive
    c. concrete
    d. centered

27. Sixteen-year-old Ellie has several minor scars as a result of an automobile accident. She is embarrassed to go in public because she believes that everyone is staring at her scars, even though they are relatively minor. Ellie's feelings
    a. suggest that the accident left deep emotional scars as well as physical scars
    b. are extreme and indicate a need for psychological counseling
    c. are typical during adolescence as a teenager tends to believe that others are as preoccupied with her as she herself is
    d. should be ignored

28. Conflict with parents
    a. generally decreases throughout adolescence
    b. generally increases during early adolescence and lessens during late adolescence
    c. does not typically increase or decrease during adolescence
    d. reaches a peak during late adolescence

29. During adolescence
    a. there is a decreased interest in peer groups, organizations, and teams
    b. there is a strong pressure to conform to peers
    c. there is a strong pressure to conform to parents
    d. there is a decreased push for autonomy

30. According to Erikson, adolescents are dealing with the issue of
    a. intimacy vs. isolation
    b. integrity vs. despair
    c. identity vs. identity confusion
    d. industry vs. inferiority

Childhood and Adolescence Review Answers

1. a
2. b
3. c
4. b
5. b
6. a
7. d
8. c
9. b
10. c
11. d
12. d
13. b
14. c
15. b
16. b
17. d
18. c
19. a
20. b
21. d
22. c
23. a
24. c
25. d
26. a
27. c
28. b
29. b
30. c

SECTION V   ADULTHOOD AND DEATH AND DYING CONCEPT REVIEW

Early Adulthood Review (18-21 to 39 years)

I. **Physical development**
   A. **Physical performance**
      1. Peaks of physical strength and speed occur in the 20s
      2. Physical performance begins to decline in the 30s
      3. Muscle tone and strength begin to decline in the 30s
      4. In the mid to late 20s, fatty tissue increases
   B. **Sensory systems**
      1. Show little change during early adulthood
      2. Lens of eye loses some elasticity and isn't able to focus quite as well as in adolescence
      3. Hearing peaks in adolescence, remains constant during the first part of early adulthood, and then begins to decline toward the end of early adulthood
   C. **Health**
      1. Healthiest time of life
      2. Fewer colds and respiratory problems than in childhood
      3. Few chronic health problems
   D. **Metabolism**
      1. **Basal metabolism rate**, the minimum amount of energy an individual uses in a resting state, declines gradually during adulthood
      2. To maintain weight in adulthood, have to reduce food intake
   E. **Causes of death**
      1. Accidents, suicide, and homicide are the leading causes of death among adults aged 25 to 34
      2. AIDS accounts for 13% of the deaths between ages 25 and 34
II. **Cognitive development**
   A. According to Piaget, adolescents and adults think in the same formal operational way
   B. Other developmentalists suggest that adult thinking tends to be more pragmatic than adolescent thinking, that is, adults better understand reality's constraints
   C. **Schaie's** cognitive stages of adulthood focus on how adults progress beyond adolescents in their *use* of intelligence (Schaie, 1977)
      1. The **achieving stage** is Schaie's stage of early adulthood
      2. Involves the application of intelligence to situations that have profound consequences for achieving long-term goals, such as those involving careers and knowledge
      3. Young adults need to master the cognitive skills needed to monitor their own behavior and to achieve independence
   D. **Career development**
      1. Young people should explore a variety of career options
      2. **Super's career self-concept theory** states that the individual's self-concept plays a central role in career choice (Super, 1976)
      3. **Supers career self-concept theory stages**
         a. **Crystallization**
            (1) 14-18 years
            (2) Develop ideas about work that mesh with their already existing global self-concept
         b. **Specification**
            (1) 18-22 years
            (2) Narrow their career choices and initiate behavior that enables them to enter some type of career

      c.   **Implementation**
          (1) 21-24 years
          (2) Education or training is completed and the individual enters the world of work
      d.   **Stabilization**
          (1) 25-35 years
          (2) The decision about a specific, appropriate career is made
      e.   **Consolidation**
          (1) After 35 years
          (2) Individuals seek to advance their careers and reach higher-status positions

4. **Women and work**
   a. The number of women in the work force has increased dramatically in recent years
   b. Women have increased their presence in occupations previously dominated by men
   c. Women's work patterns are more variable than men's
   d. Women are less likely than men to work continuously through their adult lives, for the majority of women some form of interrupted pattern is the norm, mainly due to taking time off to bear and rear children

III. Socioemotional development

A. **Criteria that signal the end of youth and the beginning of adulthood**
   1. Economic independence
   2. Independent decision making

B. **Erikson's sixth stage of psychosocial development** (Erikson, 1968)
   1. **Intimacy vs. isolation (early adulthood)**
      a. If young adults form healthy friendships and an intimate relationship with another individual, intimacy will be achieved
      b. If intimacy not established, isolation will result

C. **Gould's transformations of adulthood** (Gould, 1994)
   1. **16 to 18:** Desire to escape parental control
   2. **18 to 22:** Leaving the family; peer group orientation
   3. **22 to 28:** Assuming new roles; developing independence; commitment to a career and to children
   4. **29 to 34:** Beginning to feel stuck with responsibilities; questioning self; role confusion; marriage and career vulnerable to dissatisfaction

D. **Levinson's season's of a man's life** (Levinson, 1978)
   1. **Developmental tasks of early adulthood**
      a. Exploring the possibilities for adult living
      b. Developing a stable life structure
   2. **During the late teens**, transition from dependence to independence should occur
   3. **During the 20s**, individuals should form a "dream" for their life, involving goals for career and marriage, and develop a relationship with a mentor
   4. **From 28 to 33**, a transition time of reevaluating goals and progress towards reaching goals
   5. **From 33 to 39**, a stable period focused on family and career development
   6. Levinson's theory was originally based on a small group of men
   7. Later studies of women have shown than women go through similar sequences of stages but with quite different timing of life events
   8. Women's "dreams" are likely to differ from men's, and women are less likely than men to have a mentor

E. **Kohlberg's third level of moral reasoning: Postconventional reasoning** (Kohlberg, 1976)
   1. Morality is completely internalized and not based on others' standards
   2. The person recognizes alternative moral courses, explores the options, and then decides on a personal moral code
   3. By early adulthood, a small number of people reason in postconventional ways

4. **Two postconventional stages**
    a. **Stage 5. Community rights versus individual rights**
        (1) The person understands that values and laws are relative and that standards may vary from one person to another
        (2) The person recognizes that laws are important for society but knows that laws can be changed
        (3) The person believes that some values, such as liberty, are more important than the law
    b. **Stage 6. Universal ethical principles**
        (1) Persons have developed a moral standard based on universal human rights
        (2) When faced with a conflict between law and conscience, the person will follow conscience, even though the decision might involve personal risk
5. **Criticisms of Kohlberg's theory**
    a. Puts too much emphasis on moral thought and not enough on moral behavior
    b. Culturally biased; moral reasoning is culture-specific and Kohlberg's theory does not recognize some forms of high-level reasoning common to certain cultural groups
    c. Gilligan (1982) has criticized Kohlberg's theory on the basis of that it does not adequately reflect relationships and concern for others, a concern more common among women than men

F. **Marriage**
    1. More adults are remaining single longer in the 1990s than in previous years
    2. Average age at marriage is increasing
    3. Divorce rate, which increased dramatically in the 1970s, is beginning to slow down
    4. Proportion of women who never marry has stayed at 7% throughout the 20th century
    5. The age at which individuals marry, expectations about what the marriage will be like, and the developmental course of the marriage varies across historical time and across cultures
    6. Unrealistic expectations about marriage may be related to the high divorce rate in the U.S.

G. **Parenthood**
    1. Parenting consists of a number of interpersonal skills and emotional demands, yet there is little in the way of formal education for this task
    2. Most parents learn parenting tasks from their own parents -- some they accept, some they discard
    3. Currently, there is a tendency to have fewer children, and to have them later
    4. Giving birth to fewer children and reduced demands of child care have resulted in changes
        a. As a result of the increase in working women, there is less maternal investment in the child's development
        b. Men are apt to invest a greater amount of time in fathering than they did in the past
        c. Parental care in the home is often supplemented by institutional care (e.g., day care)

Middle Adulthood Review (40 to 64 years)

I. **Physical development**
    A. Middle adulthood is a time of general decline in physical fitness
    B. Appearance shows signs of aging including graying hair, facial wrinkles, sagging bodies; middle-aged adults may try in various ways to make themselves look younger
    C. **Height** may begin to decrease slightly as disks between the vertebrae of the spine deteriorate
    D. **Weight**
        1. Basal metabolism rate continues to decline
        2. Being overweight is a critical problem during middle adulthood
        3. Obesity increases the probability of many health problems including hypertension and digestive disorders

E. **Senses**
   1. **Vision**
      a. Ability to focus declines sharply between 40 and 59
      b. Middle-aged individuals especially likely to have difficulty viewing close objects
   2. **Hearing**
      a. May start to decline by age 40
      b. Sensitivity to high frequency pitches usually declines first
      c. Sensitivity to low frequency sounds does not decline much in middle adulthood
      d. Males usually experience greater hearing losses sooner than females
F. **Health status**
   1. Health status becomes a major concern in middle adulthood
   2. **Cardiovascular disease**
      a. Leading cause of death during middle adulthood
      b. Death rate from cardiovascular disease has been dropping over the last twenty years
      c. **Risk factors**
         (1) High blood pressure
         (2) Smoking
         (3) High cholesterol levels
         (4) Inactivity, lack of exercise
         (5) High-fat diet
         (6) Obesity
         (7) Family history of heart disease
   3. **Cancer**
      a. Second leading cause of death during middle adulthood
      b. Incidence of cancer goes up with age
      c. Rate of cancer death has increased in recent decades
      d. **Risk factors**
         (1) Smoking
         (2) Inactivity is associated with some forms of cancer, such as colon cancer
         (3) High-fat diet may increase risk
         (4) High-fiber diet may reduce risk
         (5) Greater weight associated with increased risk of some forms of cancer, such as breast cancer
         (6) Family history of cancer is related to some forms of cancer
   4. **Life-style and personality factors are related to health**
G. **Reproductive systems**
   1. **Females**
      a. **Menopause**, the cessation of a woman's menstrual periods and the loss of childbearing capability, usually occurs in the late forties or early fifties
      b. There is a dramatic decline in the production of estrogen by the ovaries
      c. Some women report uncomfortable symptoms such as "hot flashes", nausea, fatigue, rapid heartbeat, depression, and irritability during menopause
      d. Menopause does not produce psychological problems or physical problems for the majority of women
      e. Hormone replacement therapy may be beneficial for some women
   2. **Males**
      a. Testosterone production gradually declines
      b. Males do not lose their fertility during middle adulthood
      c. Erections are less full and less frequent
   3. Sexual activity usually occurs on a less frequent basis than during early adulthood

II. Cognitive development
  A. **Schaie's two cognitive stages of middle adulthood** (Schaie, 1977)
    1. **Responsibility stage**
        a. Often begins in early adulthood and extends into middle adulthood
        b. Occurs when the family is established and attention is given to needs of spouse and offspring
        c. Extensions of cognitive skills are needed as the individual's career develops and responsibility for others arises on the job and in the community
    2. **Executive stage**
        a. The individual develops an understanding of how societal organizations work and the complex relationships that are involved
        b. May become leaders in business, church, community, etc.
  B. **Career**
    1. Work satisfaction increases throughout career life
    2. By the 40s, most men reach career ladder peak
    3. When women have discontinuous work paths, they may still be working on establishing careers during middle adulthood
III. Socioemotional development
  A. **Erikson's seventh stage of socioemotional development** (Erikson, 1968)
    1. **Generativity vs. stagnation (middle adulthood)**
    2. Generativity involves adults' plans for what they hope to do to leave a legacy of themselves to the next generation
    3. Generativity can occur through the parent role, work role, or community role
    4. Stagnation occurs when adults feel they have done nothing for the next generation
  B. **Gould's transformations in adult development** (Gould, 1978)
    1. **35-43 years:** Begin to feel an urgency that our lives are speeding by; awareness of time limitations for achieving life's goals; realignment of life's goals
    2. **43-53 years:** Settling down; acceptance of one's life
    3. **53-60 years:** More tolerance; acceptance of the past; less negativism; general mellowing
  C. **Levinson's seasons of a man's life** (Levinson, 1978)
    1. **Middle adulthood conflicts**
        a. Being young versus being old
        b. Being destructive versus being constructive
        c. Being masculine versus being feminine
        d. Being attached to others versus being separated from them
    2. **Mid-life transition** occurs at 40 to 45 years of age and is a time of questioning and reevaluating many aspects of one's life
    3. Mid-life transition is followed by a relatively stable period
  D. Middle-aged adults are referred to as the "**sandwich generation**" because of being squeezed by demands caused by having elderly, aging parents and by being parents of adolescents or young adults
  E. Known as the "**command generation**" because they often assume roles of importance in the community during middle age
  F. **Empty nest syndrome**
    1. States that marital satisfaction will decrease because parents derive considerable satisfaction from their children, and therefore, the children's departure will leave parents with empty feelings
    2. While the empty nest syndrome may hold true for some parents who live vicariously through their children, the empty nest usually does not lower marital satisfaction
    3. Marital satisfaction typically increases in the post-childrearing years
  G. **Tasks of middle adulthood**
    1. Need to adjust to the physiological changes of aging
    2. Need to maintain satisfactory status in career
    3. Need to begin preparing for retirement, develop leisure tasks

Late Adulthood Review (65 years and up)

I. **Physical development**
   A. **Life expectancy and life span**
      1. **Maximum life span** is the upper boundary of life, the maximum number of years an individual can live; about 120 years
      2. **Life expectancy** is the number of years that will probably be lived by the average person born in a particular year
         a. Life expectancy for males in the U.S. is 72 years of age
         b. Life expectancy for females in the U.S. is 78 years of age
         c. More males than females are born, but beginning at age 25 females outnumber males
         d. By the time adults are 75 years of age, more than 61 percent are female
         e. For adults 85 years and over, about 70 percent are female
         f. Sex differences in life expectancy are due to both social and biological factors
   B. **Subperiods of late adulthood**
      1. **Young-old:** 65 to 74 years of age
      2. **Middle-old:** 75 to 84 years of age
      3. **Oldest-old:** 85 years and up
         a. Oldest-old are more likely to be female
         b. Have a higher rate of morbidity and a greater incidence of disability than the young-old
         c. More likely to be living in institutions
         d. Less likely to be married
         e. Their needs, capacities, and resources are often different from those of the young- and middle-old
         f. A substantial portion of the oldest old function effectively
   C. Older adults are a very heterogeneous group with some functioning independently very effectively while others are very dependent on others
   D. **Biological theories of aging**
      1. **Microbiological theories** look within the body's cells to explain aging
         a. **Cellular garbage:** As cells age, they have more difficulty disposing of their wastes; cellular functioning becomes slower because of the crowding by wastes
         b. **Cross-linkage:** As cells age, their molecules can become linked or attached to each other in ways that stop biochemical cycles and disrupt cell functioning
         c. **Cellular clock:** Body cells can divide only a limited number of times
         d. **Free radical:** Aging is a result of cell damage caused by oxygen-free radicals, which are produced both by the body's own metabolism and by environmental factors such as smoking, pollution, and bad chemicals in the diet; vitamin supplements containing antioxidants (such as vitamin E and beta-carotene) are thought to counteract the cell damage caused by free radicals
      2. **Macrobiological theories** examine aging at a more global level of analysis than the cell
         a. **Immune system:** Immune system loses its ability to recognize bacteria and other invaders such as cancer cells; also starts to attack the body's own healthy cells
         b. **Hypothalamus, pituitary:** Aging timer is located in the brain; related to "aging" hormone
         c. **Homeostasis, organ reserve:** Aging is related to a decline in the body's organ reserve
         d. **Wear-and-tear:** Body is like a machine and wears out with age

E. **Physical changes**
1. **Brain and nervous system**
    a. The number of neurons in the brain decreases
    b. Dendritic growth may compensate for neuron loss through the 70s but not when individuals reach their 90s
    c. A myth about aging is that all older adults lose a majority of their brain cells and experience dramatic deterioration in brain functioning
2. **The senses**
    a. **Vision**
        (1) Decline in vision becomes more pronounced
        (2) Night driving becomes more difficult because of reduced glare tolerance
        (3) Dark adaptation is slower
        (4) Visual field becomes smaller
        (5) Reduction in the quality or intensity of light reaching the retina
    b. **Hearing**
        (1) By 75 to 79 years of age, 75% of individuals experience some type of hearing problem
        (2) Some hearing problems may be corrected by hearing aids
    c. Become less sensitive to **taste** and **smell**
3. **Lung capacity** drops 40 percent between the ages of 40 and 80; lungs lose elasticity
4. **Arteriosclerotic** with decreased elasticity of blood vessels
5. Decreased **cardiac** output
6. **Sexuality**
    a. Sexuality can be lifelong
    b. Orgasm in males becomes less frequent
7. **Reaction time** slows
8. Decreased **muscle tone, strength**
F. **Health problems**
1. **Chronic disorders**, which are characterized by a slow onset and a long duration, rarely develop in early adulthood, increase during middle adulthood, and become common in late adulthood
2. **Arthritis**
    a. The most common chronic disorder of late adulthood
    b. An inflammation of the joints accompanied by pain, stiffness, and movement problems
3. **Osteoporosis**
    a. An aging disorder involving an extensive loss of bone tissue
    b. Women are especially vulnerable to osteoporosis
    c. Leading cause of broken bones in women
    d. Related to deficiencies in calcium, vitamin D, estrogen depletion, and lack of exercise
4. **Other common chronic conditions** include heart conditions, sinus problems, arteriosclerosis, diabetes, and asthma
5. **Nearly three-fourths of all older adults die of heart disease, cancer, or cerebrovascular disease**
G. **Exercise** is beneficial for health in late adulthood
H. **A well-balanced, low-fat diet** is recommended
II. **Cognitive development**
A. **Schaie's cognitive stage of late adulthood: Reintegrative stage (late adulthood)** (Schaie, 1977)
1. Involves older adults choosing to focus their energy on the tasks and activities that have meaning for them
2. Acquisition and application of knowledge is related to their interests, attitudes, and values

B. **Cognitive changes**
   1. **Speed of processing information** declines in late adulthood
   2. Older adults are less efficient than younger adults at retrieving information from **memory**
   3. Poor health is associated with decreased performance on intelligence tests during late adulthood
   4. Exercise is related to improved cognitive functioning among older adults
C. **Phases of retirement** (Atchley, 1976): Individuals retire at different ages and for different reasons, so there is no particular timing or sequencing of the phases of retirement
   1. **Remote phase:** Doing little to prepare for retirement
   2. **Near phase:** Worker begins to participate in a preretirement program
   3. **Honeymoon phase:** Many individuals feel euphoric immediately after retirement
   4. **Disenchantment phase:** Sometimes older adults discover that their preretirement fantasies about retirement were unrealistic
   5. **Reorientation phase:** Retirees take stock, pull themselves together, and develop more realistic life alternatives
   6. **Stability phase:** Adults have decided upon a set criteria for evaluating choices in retirement and how they will perform once they have made these choices
   7. **Termination phase:** The retirement role is replaced by the sick or dependent role because the older adult can no longer function autonomously and be self-sufficient
D. **Dementia**
   1. Alzheimer's disease is the most common cause of dementia
   2. Vascular disorders are the second most common cause
   3. **Alzheimer's disease**
      a. A progressive, irreversible brain disorder characterized by gradual deterioration of memory, reasoning, language, and eventually physical functioning; usually fatal in about 5 years
      b. Affects 2 to 4% of the population over 65 years of age
      c. More common in females than in males
      d. Difficult to diagnose and to know when it begins
      e. Seems to have a genetic component but is triggered by something in the environment
      f. Brains of Alzheimer's patients have increased levels of neuritic plaque
      g. The neurotransmitter acetylcholine, which is important in memory and the motor control of muscles, appears to be involved in Alzheimer's
      h. Individuals with Alzheimer's need a safe, structured, consistent environment

III. **Socioemotional development**
   A. **Social theories of aging**
      1. **Disengagement theory** (Cumming & Henry, 1961)
         a. As older adults slow down they gradually withdraw from society
         b. Older adults develop an increasing self-preoccupation, lessen emotional ties with others, and show a decreasing interest in society's affairs
         c. Disengagement theory describes what sometimes happens with older adults but not what should happen for higher life satisfaction
      2. **Activity theory**
         a. The more active and involved older adults are, the less likely they will age and the more likely they will be satisfied with their lives
         b. Suggests that individuals should continue their middle adulthood roles through late adulthood
         c. If roles are taken away from them, they should find substitute roles that keep them active and involved in society
      3. **Social breakdown-reconstruction theory** (Kuypers & Bengston, 1973)
         a. Aging is promoted through negative psychological functioning brought about by negative societal views of older adults and inadequate provision of services for them
         b. Social reconstruction can occur by changing society's view of older adults and by providing adequate support systems for them

       c.   Older adults' capabilities and competence are far greater than society has acknowledged in the past

B. **Ageism**
1. Prejudice against older adults
2. Older adults may not be hired for new jobs because older adults are stereotyped as too rigid or feebleminded
3. Older adults may be shunned socially because older adults are stereotyped as senile or boring

C. **Erikson's eighth stage of psychosocial development: Integrity vs. despair (late adulthood)** (Erikson, 1968)
1. During the later years, adults look back at what they have done with their lives
2. If retrospective looks and reminiscence reveals a picture of a life well spent, the older adult will be satisfied and achieve integrity
3. If the older adult looks back and feels doubt, gloom, and despair over the worth, a feeling of despair will result

D. **Peck's three developmental tasks of late adulthood** (Peck, 1968)
1. **Differentiation vs. role preoccupation:** Older adults must redefine their worth in terms of something other than work role
2. **Body transcendence vs. body preoccupation:** Older adults must cope with declining physical well-being
3. **Ego transcendence vs. ego preoccupation:** Older adults must recognize that while death is inevitable and probably not too far away, they feel at ease with themselves by realizing that they have contributed to the future through the competent rearing of their children or through their vocation and ideas

E. **Other adjustments of late adulthood**
1. Living on a reduced income; women are more likely than men to experience poverty during late adulthood
2. Death of spouse and friends
3. Decreased physical abilities

F. **Life review** is a common theme in theories of personality development in late adulthood; life review involves looking back at one's life experiences and evaluating them

G. **Life satisfaction** is psychological well-being in general or satisfaction with life as a whole
1. Older adults with adequate income are more likely to be satisfied with their lives than older adults with less adequate income
2. Healthy older adults are more likely than unhealthy older adults to have high life satisfaction
3. An active life-style is associated with high life satisfaction
4. Older adults with an extended social network of friends and family are more likely to be satisfied with their lives
5. A close attachment to one or more individuals is associated with high life satisfaction

H. **The selective optimization with compensation model** suggests that successful aging is related to three factors (Baltes & Baltes, 1990)
1. **Selection:** In old age there is a reduced capacity and loss of functioning, which mandate a reduction of performance in most domains of life
2. **Optimization:** It is possible to maintain performance in some area by practice and the use of new technologies
3. **Compensation:** Becomes relevant when life tasks require a level of capacity beyond the current level of the older adult's performance potential

I. **Suicide**
  1. Nearly 25% of individuals who commit suicide in the United States are over 65 years of age
  2. **Risk factors** related to suicide in older adults
      a. Living along
      b. Being male
      c. Losing a spouse
      d. Experiencing failing health
J. **Elder abuse**
  1. Accurate estimates of the incidence of elder abuse are difficult to obtain
  2. **Types of abuse**
      a. Physical abuse
      b. Chronic verbal abuse
      c. Neglect
  3. **Victim characteristics**
      a. Those over 75 are more likely to be abused
      b. Those in poor physical or mental health are more likely to be abused
      c. Loyal or dependent elders may be reluctant to report abuse
      d. Those who stoically accept adversity may be more likely to tolerate abuse
      e. Older people with difficult personalities may be more likely to be abused
  4. **Abuser characteristics**
      a. Spouse of the victim is the most frequent perpetrator of abuse
      b. Caregivers who are financially dependent on the older person
      c. Caregivers who drink, use drugs, or are mentally incompetent
      d. Experiencing stress due to economic problems
      e. Ignorance of older person's needs
  5. **Preventing elder abuse**
      a. Screen caregiving individuals
      b. Clearly define responsibilities and methods for reporting elder abuse
      c. Change violent, ageist societal attitudes in the U.S.
      d. Reduce factors, such as unemployment and poverty, that increase the chances of family dysfunction

Death and Dying Review

I. **Definitions of death**
  A. **Brain death**
      1. A neurological definition of death which states that a person is brain dead when all electrical activity of the brain has ceased for a specified period of time
      2. A flat EEG (electroencephalogram) recording for a specified period of time is one criterion of brain death
  B. **Euthanasia:** The act of painlessly putting to death persons who are suffering from an incurable disease or severe disability; sometimes called "mercy killing"
      1. **Active euthanasia:** Occurs when death is induced by a deliberate attempt to end a person's life, such as in the injection of a lethal dose of a drug
      2. **Passive euthanasia:** Occurs when a person is allowed to die by withholding an available treatment, for example, withdrawing a life-sustaining therapeutic device

II. **Developmental changes in understanding death and attitudes toward death**
- A. **Newborn to 3 years**
  1. Infants do not understand the concept of death
  2. As they develop attachment to a caregiver, they can experience loss or separation and an accompanying anxiety
- B. **Children 3 to 5 years**
  1. Have little or no idea of what death really means
  2. Confuse death with sleep
  3. Rarely get upset by being told that a person has died
  4. Believe the dead can be brought back to life by magic or by giving them food or medical treatment
  5. Often believe that only people who want to die, or who are bad or careless, actually die
  6. May blame themselves for the death of someone they knew well, illogically reasoning that the event may have happened because they disobeyed the person who died
- C. **Middle and late childhood**
  1. Children 6 to 9 believe that death exists but only happens to some people
  2. Children 9 years and older recognize that death is final and universal
  3. Death should be discussed honestly with children
  4. Death is rarely discussed in our society, but death should not be treated as an unmentionable topic
- D. **Adolescence**
  1. Death is regarded as something very remote
  2. The subject of death may be avoided, glossed over, kidded about, or controlled by a cool, spectatorlike orientation
  3. Some adolescents do show a concern for death, trying to understand its meaning and confront their own death
  4. Notions of death become more abstract
  5. Develop religious and philosophical views about the nature of death and whether there is life after death
- E. **Adulthood**
  1. An increased consciousness about death accompanies individuals' awareness that they are aging, which usually intensifies in middle adulthood
  2. Middle-aged adults fear death more than young adults or older adults do
  3. Older adults think about death more and talk about it more than do young and middle-aged adults
  4. Older adults have more direct experience with death as their friends and relatives become ill and die
  5. Older adults examine the meaning of life and death more frequently than younger adults
  6. Death may be less emotionally painful for older adults because they are more likely to have had their spouses die and are less likely to have unfinished business

III. **Kübler-Ross's stages of dying** (Kübler-Ross, 1969): These stages are based on terminally ill patients; according to Kübler-Ross going through these five stages is the optimal way to face death; others have suggested that people tend to go through the stages in different orders, skip stages, repeat stages, and generally believe that adaptation does not require people to go through the stages in the order described by Kübler-Ross
- A. **Denial and isolation**: Individual denies that death is really going to take place
- B. **Anger**: The dying person recognizes that denial can no longer be maintained; denial often gives way to anger, resentment, rage, and envy
- C. **Bargaining**: Person develops the hope that death can somehow be postponed or delayed
- D. **Depression**: The dying person comes to accept the certainty of death; at this point a period of depression or preparatory grief may appear
- E. **Acceptance**: The person develops a sense of peace; an acceptance of one's fate; and, in many cases, a desire to be left alone

IV. **Stages of grief:** People do not necessarily go through these stages in order; many developmentalists believe it is better to understand grief's dimensions rather than stages (Averill, 1968)

A. **Stage 1: Shock and disbelief**
1. Survivor feels shock, disbelief, and numbness, often weeping or becoming easily agitated
2. Occurs just after the death and lasts for 1 to 3 days

B. **Stage 2: Developing awareness**
1. Painful longing for the dead, memories and visual images of the deceased, sadness, insomnia, irritability, and restlessness
2. May experience physical symptoms such as nausea, vomiting, loss of appetite, crying, anger
3. Begins not long after the death and often peaks in the second to fourth weeks following the death
4. May subside after several months, although it can persist for 1 to 2 years

C. **Stage 3: Resolution**
1. Marked by a resumption of ordinary activities, a greater probability of recalling pleasant memories about the deceased, and the establishment of new relationships with others
2. Acceptance occurs
3. Usually appears within a year after the death

Adulthood and Death Review Questions

Mr. Mahoney is 65 years old and is active in the physically demanding business of manufacturing and installing basketball goals. At the urging of his wife, who thinks he is too old to keep working so hard, he is now visiting his physician for a routine physical examination to evaluate his physical condition, and to find out more about what he should expect to happen to his physical and mental abilities as he gets older.

Questions 1-8 refer to the above situation.

1. Mrs. Mahoney is concerned that all the physical exercise Mr. Mahoney is getting on the job is going to cause him to age faster, just like a car that is driven a lot of miles. Mrs. Mahoney subscribes to a _____ biological theory of aging.
   a. cross-linkage
   b. cellular clock
   c. free radical
   d. wear-and-tear

2. The nurse could tell Mr. and Mrs. Mahoney that physical exercise during late adulthood is generally associated with
   a. lower levels of physical and cognitive functioning
   b. higher levels of physical and cognitive functioning
   c. decreased physical functioning and increased cognitive functioning
   d. increased physical functioning and decreased cognitive functioning

3. Mr. Mahoney admits that he has noticed some changes in his vision. What kind of change is he most likely to see in late adulthood?
   a. reduced glare tolerance
   b. faster dark adaptation
   c. larger visual field
   d. increased intensity of light reaching the retina

4. Mr. Mahoney wants to make sure he retires before he becomes senile. He's heard that all older adults eventually become senile. What can the nurse tell him about cognitive deterioration during late adulthood?
   a. Severe cognitive deterioration is a pathological condition, not a part of normal aging, is most often caused by Alzheimer's Disease, and does not happen to all old people.
   b. The incidence of senility is no greater in the elderly population than in the total adult population.
   c. Senility is an inevitable part of aging, with an average onset of 75 years of age
   d. The only way he will become senile is if senility runs in his family, so he should look to his parents and grandparents to see what will happen to himself as he ages.

5. Mr. Mahoney worked hard his whole life and never took the time to develop any interests outside of work. He finds it hard to imagine what life would be like without work and is concerned about feeling worthless if he retires. Mr. Mahoney is facing the developmental task of
   a. ego transcendence vs. ego preoccupation
   b. body transcendence vs. body preoccupation
   c. differentiation vs. role preoccupation
   d. mental flexibility vs. rigidity

6. According to the selective optimization with compensation model, Mr. Mahoney would be able to age successfully if he would
   a. do less of the physically demanding aspects of his job as his physical capacity declines and look into new techniques of installing goals that require less physical strength
   b. continue to perform all aspects of his job and just physically work harder at it
   c. realize that he should be able continue in his job as he has in the past with no changes necessary as long as he has the right mental attitude
   d. retire immediately and find something totally different to occupy his time

7. When Mr. Mahoney looks back on his life, he feels pleased about the way his eight children turned out, happy to have such a caring and concerned wife, and proud that one of his sons has joined him in the basketball goal business. Mr. Mahoney appears to have resolved Erikson's eighth developmental stage with a feeling of
   a. autonomy
   b. intimacy
   c. integrity
   d. identity

8. Mr. and Mrs. Mahoney have had a very satisfactory sex life up until now, and Mr. Mahoney is a little worried that as he gets older, he will no longer be capable of sexual intercourse. What could the nurse tell him about sexuality in late adulthood?
   a. Sexual relations usually continue throughout late adulthood with no changes in intensity or frequency.
   b. Although male orgasms may become less frequent, sexual relations can continue throughout late adulthood.
   c. Although sexual relations are physically possible throughout late adulthood, most elderly adults lose interest in sex after the late sixties.
   d. Sexual capabilities decrease sharply during late adulthood, with most elderly adults being incapable of sexual functioning.

9. The peak of physical strength and speed occurs during
   a. adolescence
   b. early adulthood
   c. middle adulthood
   d. late adulthood

10. During early adulthood, sensory systems
    a. show little change
    b. improve significantly
    c. show dramatic decreases in functioning
    d. vary in their functioning with hearing showing no decline but visual systems showing marked decline

11. The healthiest time of life is
    a. childhood
    b. early adulthood
    c. middle adulthood
    d. late adulthood

12. Basal metabolism rate
    a. increases sharply during adulthood
    b. increases slightly during adulthood
    c. stays the same during adulthood
    d. gradually declines during adulthood

13. Compared to adolescent thinking, adult thinking tends to be more
    a. abstract
    b. idealistic
    c. pragmatic
    d. logical

14. During early adulthood, individuals are focused on
    a. acquiring knowledge
    b. applying intelligence to achieve career goals
    c. applying intelligence to take care of responsibilities to others
    d. understanding how societal organizations work

15. Adrian is 22 years old. In terms of career development, he is likely to be focusing on
    a. developing ideas about careers that fit with his self-concept
    b. making a decision about a specific, appropriate career
    c. narrowing his career choices, completing his education, and entering the world of work
    d. seeking to advance his career and reach a higher-status position

16. During early adulthood, individuals are focused on the developmental task of
    a. identity vs. identity confusion
    b. generativity vs. stagnation
    c. integrity vs. despair
    d. intimacy vs. isolation

17. Will is 32 years of age. Gould's transformations to adulthood suggest that Will is likely to be
    a. trying to escape parental control
    b. leaving the family and orienting on peer groups
    c. assuming new roles and committing himself to a career
    d. beginning to feel stuck with responsibilities and questioning himself

18. According to Levinson's theory of the seasons of a man's life, during the 20s adults should be
    a. forming a dream about career and marriage goals for their adult life
    b. going through a transition time of reevaluating goals
    c. be in a stable period focused on family and career development
    d. making the transition from dependence to independence

19. During middle adulthood
    a. being overweight is not usually much of a problem
    b. visual problems involving seeing close objects are likely to develop
    c. sensitivity to low frequency sounds declines
    d. physical fitness is usually maintained

20. Menopause usually occurs
    a. in the early thirties
    b. by age 40
    c. in the late forties or early fifties
    d. in the late fifties

21. Which of the following statements concerning the reproductive systems in adult males is true?
    a. Testosterone production gradually declines during adulthood
    b. Testosterone production declines sharply during middle adulthood.
    c. Males lose their fertility during late adulthood.
    d. Erections occur at the same level of frequency throughout adulthood.

22. Adults are most likely to become leaders in business and the community during
    a. early adulthood
    b. middle adulthood
    c. late adulthood
    d. all times of adulthood

23. Erikson's developmental task of middle adulthood involves
    a. intimacy vs. isolation
    b. identity vs. identity confusion
    c. integrity vs. despair
    d. generativity vs. stagnation

24. More tolerance, less negativism, and general mellowing is characteristic of the
    a. 20s
    b. 40s
    c. 50s
    d. 70s

25. Older adults
    a. are a very homogeneous group from age 65 up
    b. show a lot of variability in functioning
    c. have relatively more acute disorders and fewer chronic disorders
    d. are too old to safely exercise

26. Cognitive functioning in late adulthood
    a. shows a decline in the speed of processing
    b. shows no memory decline except when dementia is present
    c. shows more decline on verbal tasks than on performance tasks
    d. is not related to health

27. Activity theory of aging suggests that
    a. as adults age, they should gradually withdraw from society
    b. ageism promotes successful aging
    c. the more active and involved adults are, the more likely they will be satisfied with their lives
    d. older adults' capabilities are less than society has acknowledged in the past

28. Four-year-old Ray has just been told that his great-grandmother died. Which of the following is he LEAST likely to do?
    a. become extremely upset
    b. believe that his great-grandmother is just sleeping
    c. blame himself for his great-grandmother's death
    d. believe that his great-grandmother can be brought back to life with medical treatment

29. According to Kübler-Ross's stages of dying, when an individual is first faced with the knowledge they are dying the most likely reaction is
    a. anger
    b. depression
    c. denial
    d. acceptance

30. Sometimes a dying person will somehow try to postpone or delay their death in some way. Kübler-Ross suggests that this occurs in a stage called
    a. denial
    b. bargaining
    c. depression
    d. anger

Adulthood and Death Review Answers

1. d
2. b
3. a
4. a
5. c
6. a
7. c
8. b
9. b
10. a
11. b
12. d
13. c
14. b
15. c
16. d
17. d
18. a
19. b
20. c
21. a
22. b
23. d
24. c
25. b
26. a
27. c
28. a
29. c
30. b

SECTION VI   PRACTICE TESTS

Practice Test One

1. When discussing fetal development with a pregnant client the nurse explains that
    a. if a baby is to be left-handed after birth, the structures on the left side of the embryo's body develop before those on the right side
    b. development proceeds from head to tail, so the embryo's brain, central nervous system, and heart are formed and start functioning before limb buds appear
    c. development of structures in the embryo proceeds from external to internal structures so the heart is formed and starts functioning after limb buds appear
    d. the brain and central nervous system are formed early in the embryonic period, and the right side of the brain starts functioning much earlier than the left side

2. The outermost membrane that helps form the placenta is the
    a. amnion
    b. chorion
    c. yolk sac
    d. allantois

3. The developing cells are called a fetus from the
    a. time the fetal heart is heard
    b. eighth week to the time of birth
    c. implantation of the fertilized ovum
    d. end of the second week to the onset of labor

4. The nurse understands that an ultrasound examination ordered for a pregnant client is used primarily to
    a. estimate fetal age
    b. detect mental retardation
    c. rule out congenital defects
    d. approximate fetal linear growth

5. While caring for a 6-month-old infant, it is likely that the nurse will observe the presence of the reflex called
    a. startle
    b. Babinski
    c. extrusion
    d. tonic neck

6. A newborn's total body response to noise or movement is often distressing to the parents. It is important for the nurse to teach the parents that this response is
    a. a reflexive response that indicates normal development
    b. an involuntary response that will remain for the first year of life
    c. an automatic response that may indicate that the baby is hungry
    d. a voluntary response that indicates insecurity in a new environment

7. The nurse observes a normal newborn lying in a supine position with the head turned to the side, legs and arms extended on the same side and flexed on the opposite side. This is
    a. the Moro reflex
    b. the Landau reflex
    c. a tonic neck reflex
    d. an abnormal reflex

8. The Moro reflex response is marked by
    a. extension of the arms
    b. adduction of the arms
    c. abduction and then adduction of the arms
    d. extension of the legs and fanning of the toes

9. An appropriate toy for a 3-month-old infant would be a
    a. push-pull toy
    b. metallic mirror
    c. stuffed animal
    d. large plastic ball

10. After teaching a mother about the appropriate play for an 8-month-old infant the nurse is aware that the mother needs additional teaching when the mother states that she will buy a
    a. stuffed animal
    b. play telephone
    c. hanging mobile
    d. book with textures

11. When selecting a toy for a 5-month-old infant, the nurse should avoid giving the infant
    a. brightly colored mobiles
    b. snap toys, large snap beads
    c. small rattles that the infant can hold
    d. soft, stuffed animals that the infant can hold

The Practice Tests and their Rationales come from the following sources:
Saxton, D.F. et al., *Mosby's Review Questions for NCLEX-RN*, 2d ed. 1995. St. Louis: Mosby-Year Book.

Saxton, D.F., Nugent, P.M., and Pelikan, P.K., *Mosby's Comprehensive Review of Nursing*, 15th ed. 1996. St Louis: Mosby-Year Book.

12. The nurse recognizes that behaviors typical of an 8-month-old include
    a. drinking from a cup, using the words "Mama" and "Dada," and standing alone
    b. smiling spontaneously, clasping hands, and keeping the head steady when sitting
    c. being shy with strangers, playing peek-a-boo, and standing by holding onto furniture
    d. removing some clothing, building a tower of two cubes, and stooping to pick up toys

13. An assessment of a 6-month-old infant's growth and developmental level should reveal that the infant can
    a. say, "Mama"
    b. crawl forward
    c. turn pages in a book
    d. hold a bottle without help

14. One month after abdominal surgery, a 6-month-old infant is brought to the pediatric clinic for a follow-up visit. The nurse observes the child performing all of the following tasks. The task that would be most unusual for a child of this age is
    a. putting clothespins in a plastic bottle
    b. sitting alone for brief periods in a crib
    c. playing with his toes during examination
    d. showing stranger-anxiety when the nurse approaches

15. During a well-baby visit the nurse recognizes that an 18-month-old's growth and development is within the normal range when the child
    a. climbs up the stairs
    b. pedals a tricycle easily
    c. says 150 different words
    d. builds a tower of 8 blocks

16. The primary task to be accomplished between 12 and 15 months of age is to learn to
    a. walk erect
    b. climb stairs
    c. use a spoon
    d. say simple words

17. The nurse is aware that 18-month-old children with normal hearing have usually acquired a vocabulary sufficient to enable them to communicate by
    a. pointing and grunting
    b. using at least six words
    c. make babbling sounds
    d. using complete sentences

18. The nurse, assigned to a 5 1/2- month-old girl being admitted to the hospital, understands that the infant's emotional development should make the infant
    a. cry when the nurse approaches her for the first time
    b. welcome the attention that the nurse gives her
    c. smile socially in recognition of the nurse's face
    d. cling furiously to her mother when the nurse tries to take her away

19. At the well-baby clinic, the nurse discusses the food and feeding needs of a toddler with the mother of a two-year-old. Considering a toddler's food and feeding needs the nurse should teach the mother that
    a. growth rate is increased at the age of 2 years, so the child needs more protein per unit of body size
    b. a child's energy requirements during the toddler stage are so high more calories are needed to meet them
    c. a child's normal struggle for independence at this age often involves refusal of food, but children will eat the amount they need
    d. because the child often refuses food, the mother should prepare only the food the child likes and avoid snacks between meals

20. The nurse observes a 2-year-old at play and notes that this age toddler
    a. builds houses with blocks
    b. is extremely possessive of toys
    c. attempts to stay within the lines when coloring
    d. amuses himself with a picture book for 15 minutes

21. A mother tells the nurse that each morning she offers her 24-month-old son juice and he always shakes his head and says, "No." She asks the nurse what to do, since she knows the child needs fluids. The nurse suggests that the mother
    a. distract him with some food
    b. be firm and hand him the glass
    c. let him see that he is making her angry
    d. offer him a choice of two things to drink

22. A characteristic of infants and young children who have experienced maternal deprivation is
    a. extreme activity
    b. proneness to illness
    c. responsiveness to stimuli
    d. tendency to overeating

23. According to Piaget's theory of cognitive development, a 6-month-old should be demonstrating
    a. early traces of memory
    b. beginning sense of time
    c. repetitious use of reflexes
    d. beginning of object permanence

24. The nurse is aware that the play of a 5-month-old infant is most likely to consist of
    a. picking up a rattle or toy and putting it into the mouth
    b. exploratory searching when a cuddly toy is hidden from view
    c. simultaneously kicking the legs and batting the hands in the air
    d. waving and clenching fists and dropping toys placed in the hands

25. The nurse is aware that the kind of play two-year-old children engage in is called
    a. group play
    b. parallel play
    c. dramatic play
    d. cooperative play

26. To bring about effective communication with any child, the nurse must first take into consideration the child's
    a. state of health
    b. developmental level
    c. ability at self-expression
    d. fear of authoritarian figures

27. The nurse understands that the first activity of daily living that should be taught to a developmentally disabled child is
    a. toileting
    b. dressing
    c. self feeding
    d. combing hair

28. Based on an understanding of normal preschool behavior, during hospitalization the nurse is aware that a 4-year-old will probably
    a. refuse to cooperate with nurses during the parents' absence
    b. demonstrate despair if parents do not visit at least once a week
    c. cry when the parents leave and return but not during their absence
    d. be unable to relate to peers in the playroom if there are parents present

29. A 2 1/2-year-old girl, whose older sibling has recently died, has started hitting her mother and refusing to go to bed at night. The nurse in the pediatric well-child clinic tells the mother that the toddler is probably
    a. fearful of dying in her sleep
    b. trying to get more of her mother's attention
    c. just going through the "terrible twos" developmental stage
    d. reacting appropriately to anxiety generated by the family upheaval

30. After several days on bedrest, a preschooler with the diagnosis of acute glomerulonephritis becomes demanding and will not listen to the nurses. The child was found in the playroom twice on the previous shift. To best meet the needs of this child the nurse should
    a. ask the child not to get up again and explain the reason for bedrest
    b. place soft restraints on the child when family members cannot be present
    c. have a color television set moved into the child's room as soon as possible
    d. move the child into a room with another five-year-old who has a fractured femur

31. The nurse should understand that to a preschooler, death is thought of as
    a. an end to life
    b. a reversible separation
    c. something that happens to old people
    d. a persona who takes one away from one's family

32. A four-year-old boy with acute lymphocytic leukemia is to have a bone marrow aspiration. While involving the child in therapeutic play prior to the procedure the nurse should help him understand that
    a. he needs to have a positive attitude
    b. his parents are concerned about him
    c. he did nothing to cause his present illness
    d. his problem was caused by an environmental factor

33. When evaluating a 3-year-old's developmental progress, the nurse should recognize that development is delayed when the child is unable to
    a. copy a square
    b. hop on one foot
    c. catch a ball reliably
    d. use a spoon effectively

34. A 6-year-old is hospitalized with a diagnosis of nephrotic syndrome and the child's mother asks the nurse what she should bring her child to play with during the hospitalization. Considering the child's age the nurse should suggest that the mother bring
   a. action toys such as a hula hoop
   b. stuffed animals, large puzzles, and large blocks
   c. table games, checkers, simple card games
   d. a record player, transistor radio, and children's magazines

35. The nurse is aware that the most appropriate toy for a 2 1/2-year-old would be a
   a. plastic mirror
   b. set of nesting blocks
   c. colorful hanging mobile
   d. wooden puzzle with large pieces

36. A nine-year-old who is in bed convalescing becomes very bored and irritable. The nurse plans activities that a school-aged child would like and suggests the child
   a. play chess
   b. start a collection
   c. do arithmetic puzzles
   d. watch game shows on TV

37. A young preschool boy has been on bed rest since he was admitted to the hospital. However, as he begins to feel better, he becomes interested in playing. Based on his developmental level and activity restriction, the nurse should provide him with
   a. television viewing time
   b. squeaky stuffed animals
   c. little cars and a shoebox garage
   d. simple three- or four-piece wooden puzzles

38. When talking with a 4-year-old the nurse observes that the child is shy and stutters. The nurse is aware that stuttering in a 4-year-old child is considered
   a. a sign of a delay in neural development
   b. a normal characteristic for a preschooler
   c. the result of a serious emotional problem
   d. an indication of a serious permanent impairment

39. The nurse knows that a child is performing normal developmental tasks for a 5-year-old when the child
   a. is ritualistic when playing
   b. makes up rules for a new game
   c. asks for a pacifier when uncomfortable
   d. plays near others quietly, but not with them

40. Preschool children role play. This is an important part of socialization because it
   a. encourages expression
   b. helps children think about careers
   c. teaches children about stereotypes
   d. provides guidelines for adult behavior

41. When listing all the problems of a teenaged client who has sickle cell anemia, the nurse recognizes that priority must be given to the client's
   a. restriction of movement during periods of arthralgia
   b. altered body image resulting from skeletal deformities
   c. separation from family during periods of hospitalization
   d. interruption of learning as a result of multiple hospitalizations

42. A 15-year-old insulin dependent diabetic has a history of noncompliance with therapy. The nurse is aware that the noncompliance is developmentally related to
   a. the need for attention
   b. a denial of the diabetes
   c. the struggle for identity
   d. a regression associated with illness

43. Developmentally, a 21-year-old male client who has sustained a spinal injury below the level of T6 will most likely have difficulty with
   a. mastering his environment
   b. identifying with the male role
   c. developing meaningful relationships
   d. differentiating himself from the environment

44. When correcting myths about aging, the nurse should teach that elderly people normally have
   a. periods of confusion
   b. an inflexible attitude
   c. some senile dementia
   d. a slower reaction time

45. An elderly female client tells the nurse that she read about a vitamin that may be related to aging because of its relationship to the structure of cell walls and wonders if she should be taking it. The nurse should recognize that the client is probably referring to
   a. Vitamin A
   b. Vitamin C
   c. Vitamin E
   d. Vitamin B1

46. The mental process most sensitive to deterioration with aging seems to be
    a. judgment
    b. creativity
    c. intelligence
    d. short term memory

47. When planning care for an 85-year-old newly admitted client with the diagnosis of dementia of the Alzheimer type, the nurse should remember that confusion in the elderly
    a. follows transfer to new surroundings
    b. is always progressive and will get worse
    c. is a common finding and is to be expected with aging
    d. results from brain pathology and cannot be cured or stopped

48. When developing a plan of care for an elderly client with the diagnosis of dementia the nurse should
    a. be considerate of the client's various likes and dislikes
    b. be firm in dealing with the client's attitudes and behaviors
    c. explain to the client the details of the therapeutic regimen
    d. provide consistency in carrying out nursing activities for the client

49. The nurse is aware that characteristic behavior in the initial stage of coping with dying includes
    a. crying uncontrollably
    b. criticizing medical care
    c. refusing to receive visitors
    d. asking for additional medical consultations

50. A client with cancer of the lung says to the nurse, "If I could just be free of pain for a few days, I might be able to eat more and regain strength." In reference to the stages of dying, the client indicates
    a. frustration
    b. bargaining
    c. depression
    d. rationalization

Practice Test One Answers and Rationale

1. b
    a. Both sides of the brain develop at the same time; which side of the brain becomes dominant develops later.
    b. Development proceeds in a cephalic to caudal progression.
    c. Development proceeds in a cephalic to caudal progression, not caudal to cephalic.
    d. Both sides of the brain develop and begin functioning at the same time.

2. b
    a. The amnion is the innermost lining, from which amniotic fluid is secreted.
    b. The chorion is the outermost membrane that helps form the placenta. It develops villi and, through its interaction with the endometrium, becomes part of the placenta.
    c. The yolk sac is part of the inner structure of the blastocyst and is lined by an inner layer of cells, the endoderm; it is unrelated to placental formation.
    d. The allantois is a tubular diverticulum of the posterior part of the embryo's yolk sac; it fuses with the chorion to form the placenta.

3. b
    a. The fetal heart is heard between the twelfth and twentieth weeks; the developing cells are known as a fetus at the end of the eighth week.
    b. In the first 7 to 14 days the developing ovum is known as a blastocyst; it is called an embryo until the eighth week; the developing cells are then called fetus until birth.
    c. At the time of implantation the group of developing cells is called a blastocyst.
    d. The developing cells are known as a fetus from 8 weeks until birth.

4. a
    a. Measurement of the fetal structures provides information that is useful in approximating fetal age.
    b. This test can detect only physical defects.
    c. Ultrasound can detect some, but not all, birth defects.
    d. Ultrasound is done primarily to estimate fetal age, not to approximate linear growth.

5. b
    a. This reflex, present at birth, disappears by 4 months of age.
    b. The Babinski reflex, present at birth, should remain positive throughout the first 12 months of life.
    c. Same as answer a.
    d. Same as answer a.

6. a
    a. This is a normal Moro response, which indicates an intact nervous system.
    b. This total body reaction is the Moro response, which is normally not present after the third month of life; if it persists, there may be a neurologic disturbance.
    c. The Moro response has no relation to hunger.
    d. The Moro response is an involuntary reflex to environmental stimuli.

7. c
    a. This is the startle reflex.
    b. This is a demonstration of muscle tone while held prone and suspended in midair.
    c. The tonic neck reflex (fencing position) is a spontaneous postural reflex of the newborn that may or may not be present during the first days of life; once apparent, it persists until the third month.
    d. This is a normal, expected reflex in the neonate.

8. c
    a. This is only part of the normal Moro response; it should be accompanied by abduction and spreading of the fingers.
    b. The reflex is abduction.
    c. The Moro is a sudden extension and abduction of the arms at the shoulders and spreading of the fingers, with the index finger and thumb forming the letter "C"; this is followed by flexion and adduction; the legs may weakly flex, and the infant may cry vigorously.
    d. The legs generally flex weakly.

9. b
    a. This is appropriate for a toddler.
    b. The 3-month-old infant is interested in self-recognition and playing with the baby in the mirror.
    c. Same as answer a.
    d. Same as answer a.

10. b
   a. A stuffed animal is appropriate; it promotes manipulative play.
   b. This is inappropriate for an 8-month-old; this is appropriate for a toddler to promote imitative play.
   c. A hanging mobile is appropriate; it promotes visual stimulation.
   d. A textured book is appropriate; it promotes tactile stimulation and touch discrimination.

11. b
   a. These are appropriate to stimulate visual attention.
   b. Fine motor coordination is inadequately developed to manipulate snap toys.
   c. The voluntary grasp will allow the child to hold the toy and the rattling sound will stimulate the auditory system.
   d. These stimulate the sense of touch, and, since voluntary grasp appears at about 3 to 4 months, they would be handled satisfactorily.

12. c
   a. These are typical behaviors of a 12-month-old.
   b. These are typical behaviors of a 3-month-old.
   c. These are typical behaviors of an 8-month-old.
   d. These are typical behaviors of an 18-month-old.

13. d
   a. This is a skill of older infants.
   b. Same as answer a.
   c. Same as answer a.
   d. Six-month-olds are capable of holding their bottles.

14. a
   a. This is a behavior seen in 9- to 12-month-olds; this is the most advanced behavior listed, and is the most unusual for this age.
   b. This is a coordination ability seen in 5- to 7-month-olds.
   c. This is a coordination ability seen in 3- to 5-month-olds.
   d. This is a behavior seen in 6- to 8-month-olds.

15. a
   a. This is normal developmental behavior for 18-month-olds; however, they may have trouble coming down the stairs.
   b. This is above the level of an 18-month-old child.
   c. Same as answer b.
   d. Same as answer b.

16. a
   a. Walking is the primary developmental task of this age group. The other choices are not applicable to this age group.
   b. The ability to drink from a cup is not developed until 18 months.
   c. A child learns to climb stairs at about 18 months.
   d. Learning to walk takes precedence over learning to talk; speaking is not a primary task at this age.

17. b
   a. The child with a hearing impairment communicates in this way because the child has not acquired the rudiments of language.
   b. A vocabulary consisting of six words with telegraphic-type speech is normal for this age child.
   c. Babbling is normal communication for an 8-month-old infant, even one with a moderate hearing loss.
   d. This language skill is seen in the 5-year-old child.

18. b
   a. The infant does not yet differentiate familiar faces from those of strangers.
   b. The infant has not yet recognized boundaries between herself and her mother and is not particular about who meets and resolves needs.
   c. This behavior is that of a younger infant and does not indicate recognition of a specific person but only a human face.
   d. Because the concept of self-boundaries has not yet developed, the infant does not really know or fear separation from the mother.

19. c
   a. A toddler's growth rate and energy requirements decrease in comparison to the first year of life.
   b. Same as answer a.
   c. A toddler's increasing mobility and growing independence in behavior, including food behavior, are normal aspects of psychologic development; slowed physical growth at this age requires relatively less caloric intake.
   d. Nutritious snacks between meals should be encouraged if the child is not eating adequate meals.

20. b
   a. This task is too advanced for toddlers and more accurate for preschoolers.
   b. Common developmental norms of the toddler, who is struggling for independence, are inability to share easily, egotism, egocentrism, and possessiveness.
   c. This is true of 4-year-olds.
   d. One characteristic of toddlers is their short attention span; 15 minutes is too much to expect.

21. d
   a. This will not achieve the goal of giving fluids.
   b. This will probably not be successful with a toddler; it will probably end in disaster.
   c. This will complicate the situation and further inhibit the child's willingness to take fluids.
   d. Children who are expressing negativism need to have a feeling of control. One way of achieving this within reasonable limits is for the parent or caregiver to provide a choice of two items, rather than force one onto the child.

22. b
   a. Infants who have experienced maternal deprivation are usually quiet and nonresponsive.
   b. Infants who have experienced maternal deprivation usually exhibit failure to thrive (i.e., weight below third percentile, developmental retardation, clinical signs of deprivation, and malnutrition). These physical and emotional factors predispose the infant to a variety of illnesses.
   c. Responsiveness to stimuli is limited or nonexistent.
   d. Weight below the third percentile is characteristic.

23. d
   a. This occurs between 13 and 24 months.
   b. Same as answer a.
   c. This occurs during the first several months of life.
   d. The concept of object permanence begins to develop around 6 months of age.

24. a
   a. During the oral stage, infants tend to complete the exploration of all objects by putting the objects in the mouth as a final step.
   b. Nine- to 10-month-olds play this way as they learn that objects continue to exist even though they are not visible.
   c. These are the random reflexive movements of 1- to 2-month-olds whose voluntary control of distal extremities has not developed.
   d. This is the momentary grasp reflex of neonates before the development of eye-hand-mouth coordination.

25. b
   a. This kind of play is characteristic of older children.
   b. Toddlers play individually, although side by side (parallel play).
   c. Dramatic play or acting is characteristic of older children; they assume and act out roles.
   d. Same as answer a.

26. b
   a. This might modify the approach, but knowing the child's developmental level is the most important factor.
   b. With each age-group, there are different means of communication; the approach used with a school-age child should differ from that used with a toddler or a teenager.
   c. This would be related to the child's developmental level that should be assessed first.
   d. Although children may fear authoritarian figures, this is only one aspect included in the assessment of developmental level, a more inclusive assessment.

27. c
   a. This would not be taught before self-feeding.
   b. Same as answer a.
   c. This follows the normal course of growth and development skills and is no different with a child who is mentally retarded.
   d. Same as answer a.

28. c
   a. Preschoolers usually are quite docile and cooperative because they are afraid of being totally abandoned.
   b. The child would demonstrate despair long before the week was over.
   c. Preschoolers generally have learned to cope with parents' absence; however, emotions associated with separation and perhaps anger at being left are difficult to hide when parents arrive or leave.
   d. The presence of other children's parents would be unrelated to their relationship with peers.

29. d
   a. This is incorrect because the toddler has no reality-based concept of death.
   b. This may be true, but the primary motivation for the behavior is a response to the upheaval in the family.
   c. This is false reassurance.
   d. Changes in the daily routines in the home and anxiety expressed by family members lead to anxiety in toddlers.

30. d
   a. Preschoolers have a limited ability to understand complex explanations of cause and effect; they employ concrete thinking.
   b. This will increase agitation and be punitive.
   c. Although this would provide some distraction, it is better to permit peer contacts.
   d. Preschoolers are active, sociable individuals who enjoy the company of peers and become bored when isolated.

31. b
   a. At about 9 or 10 years of age, the child develops an adult concept of death and views it as inevitable, irreversible, and universal.
   b. Death is viewed as a separation and preschoolers believe they will return to life and former activity; this is part of the fantasy world of the child.
   c. This is true for all age groups.
   d. This is true of the 6- to 7-year-old child.

32. c
   a. This is inappropriate for a 4-year-old and does not elicit feelings.
   b. This is inappropriate; it may be frightening.
   c. This will help to elicit any fantasy the child may have; it helps the child understand that treatment is not a punishment.
   d. This is not currently supported as a cause; this is an inappropriate discussion for a 4-year-old.

33. d
   a. This is a task expected of the 4- or 5-year-old.
   b. This is a task expected of the 4-year-old.
   c. Same as answer b.
   d. This is a task expected of the 3-year-old.

34. c
   a. This activity is inappropriate during the acute phase of nephrotic syndrome because it requires too much energy.
   b. These are appropriate for the toddler who is developing fine motor skills.
   c. School-age children enjoy competition, have manipulative skills, and are creative.
   d. Magazines would interest an older child who would be more proficient in reading.

35. d
   a. This is a toy suitable for the young infant.
   b. This is more appropriate for the child of 12 months who is becoming adept at motor skills.
   c. Same as answer a.
   d. A 2 1/2-year-old is capable of fitting large wooden pieces into the puzzle; this activity challenges the child's ability to recognize shapes.

36. b
   a. This is too advanced for a normal 9-year-old.
   b. School-age children have an interest in hobbies or collections of various kinds as a means of gathering information and knowledge about the world in which they live.
   c. This would not interest a 9-year-old.
   d. This would probably not interest a 9-year-old.

37. c
   a. Unless carefully selected, many shows are inappropriate and uninteresting for a 4-year-old.
   b. Although a 4-year-old may still cling to a security toy, it would not allow for expenditure of energy.
   c. This allows an active 4-year-old to move within restrictions and encourages use of the imagination.
   d. This may provide the child with rest, but this activity is too simple for this age child and will not promote development.

38. b
    a. This is not true; stuttering is common in the preschool years.
    b. Stuttering occurs because the child's advancing mental ability and level of comprehension exceed the vocabulary acquisition in the preschool child.
    c. Same as answer a.
    d. Same as answer a.

39. b
    a. Children in the middle childhood years need conformity and rituals, whether they play games or amass collections; rules to games are fixed, unvarying and rigid; knowing the rules means belonging.
    b. A 5-year-old is able to negotiate and use make believe to play.
    c. The use of a pacifier for oral satisfaction is normal for infants.
    d. Parallel play occurs in children 2 to 3 years.

40. a
    a. Role playing encourages expressions of feelings through behavior, since childrens' ability to verbalize feelings is limited.
    b. The preschooler is too young to think about careers.
    c. This may occur, but it is not a purpose of role playing.
    d. Although preschoolers may try to imitate adults, providing guidelines for adult behavior is premature.

41. b
    a. Restriction of movement is not a major problem because when the pain is relieved and the crisis is over, activity can be resumed; for the teenager, the change in body image produces greater anxiety.
    b. The teenage child is concerned with body image and fears change or mutilation of body parts; in sickle cell anemia, bones weakened because of hyperplasia and congestion of the marrow can cause lordosis and kyphosis.
    c. Teenagers can easily tolerate extended periods of separation from the family.
    d. Although this could be a concern at this time for a teenager, altered body image is a more fearful threat.

42. c
    a. This behavior is not a bid for attention, rather it is an attempt to establish an identity which is a normal developmental task of the adolescent.
    b. Although the adolescent may be using denial, denial is not developmentally related to adolescence.
    c. Striving to attain identity and independence is a task of the adolescent, and rebellion against established norms may be exhibited.
    d. This behavior is not regression; it is an attempt to attain identity by rebellion against established norms.

43. c
    a. This is a toddler's task associated with autonomy vs. shame and doubt.
    b. This is a school-ager's task associated with initiative vs. guilt.
    c. This is the young-adult task associated with intimacy vs. isolation.
    d. Same as answer a.

44. d
    a. Confusion is not a normal process of aging, but occurs for various reasons such as multiple stresses, perceptual changes, or medication side effects.
    b. The ability to be flexible has nothing to do with age, but with character.
    c. The majority of older adults do not have organic mental disease.
    d. A decrease in neuromuscular function slows reaction time.

45. c
    a. This assists in the formation of visual purple needed for night vision.
    b. This is used for formation of collagen, which is important for maintaining capillary strength, promoting wound healing, and resisting infection.
    c. Vitamin E hinders oxidative breakdown of structural lipid membranes in body tissues caused by free radicals in the cells.
    d. This is necessary for protein and fat metabolism and normal function of the nervous system.

46. d
   a. People with normal aging process show little or no change in their judgment.
   b. Creativity is not affected by aging; many people remain creative until very late in life.
   c. There is little or no intellectual deterioration; intelligence scores show no decline up to the age of 75-80.
   d. In the aged, there is a progressive atrophy of the convolutions with a decrease in the blood flow to the brain, which may produce a tendency to become forgetful, a reduction in short-term memory, and susceptibility to personality changes.

47. a
   a. A change in environment and introduction of unfamiliar stimuli precipitate confusion in the elderly client with dementia type disorders; with appropriate intervention, including frequent reorientation, confusion can be reduced.
   b. This is untrue; reality orientation can reduce confusion.
   c. This is untrue; this is a stereotype.
   d. Same as answer b.

48. d
   a. Although this helps individualize care, continuity is the priority.
   b. Some degree of flexibility by the nurse would help to individualize care.
   c. Detailed explanations will be forgotten; instructions should be simple and to the point and given when needed.
   d. Familiarity with situations and continuity add to the client's sense of security and foster trust in the relationship.

49. d
   a. If the client is crying, the client is aware of the magnitude of the situation and is past the stage of denial.
   b. Criticism that is unjust is often characteristic of the stage of anger.
   c. This is common during the depression experienced as one moves toward acceptance.
   d. Seeking other opinions to disprove the inevitable is a form of denial employed by individuals having illnesses with a poor prognosis.

50. b
   a. Frustration is a subjective experience, a feeling of being thwarted, but not one of the stages of dying.
   b. Bargaining is one of the stages of dying in which the client promises some type of desirable behavior to postpone the inevitability of death.
   c. Classified as the fourth stage, depression represents the grief experienced as the individual recognizes the inescapability of fate.
   d. Rationalization is a defense mechanism in which attempts are made to justify or explain an unacceptable action or feeling.

Practice Test Two

1. When teaching about normal childbearing and contraceptive options, the nurse explains that fertilization of the ovum by the sperm occurs when
    a. the male sperm count is high
    b. the ovum reaches the endometrium of the uterus
    c. one sperm successfully penetrates the wall of the ovum
    d. the sperm prevents the ovum from moving along the tube

2. The inner membrane that provides a fluid medium for the embryo is the
    a. funis
    b. amnion
    c. chorion
    d. yolk sac

3. First fetal movements felt by the mother are known as
    a. lightening
    b. quickening
    c. ballottement
    d. engagement

4. In prenatal development, growth is most rapid in the
    a. first trimester
    b. third trimester
    c. second trimester
    d. implantation period

5. To meet a major developmental need of a newborn in the immediate postoperative period the nurse should
    a. give the infant a pacifier
    b. put a mobile over the infant's crib
    c. provide the infant with a soft cuddly toy
    d. warm the infant's formula before feeding

6. To best assist new parents to understand the unique characteristics of a newborn, the nurse should discuss with them the
    a. infant's response to routine feeding schedules
    b. testing of the normal newborn's auditory acuity
    c. newborn's behaviors and states of wakefulness
    d. importance of reading about parent-infant bonding

7. The nurse may best obtain a Moro reflex by
    a. grasping the infant's hand
    b. stimulating the infant's feet
    c. creating a loud noise suddenly
    d. changing the infant's equilibrium

8. When performing a developmental appraisal on a 6-month-old infant, the observation that would be most important to the nurse in light of a diagnosis of hydrocephalus would be
    a. head lag
    b. inability to sit unsupported
    c. presence of the Babinski reflex
    d. absence of Moro, tonic neck, and grasp reflexes

9. The most appropriate toys for a 6-month-old infant would be
    a. push-pull toys
    b. wooden blocks
    c. soft stuffed animals
    d. shape-matching toys

10. A one-year-old visits the hospital playroom. The toy selected and used that would indicate an appropriate growth and developmental level would be a
    a. picture book
    b. rocking horse
    c. stuffed animal
    d. plastic toy that squeaks

11. To promote growth and development, the nurse instructs the mother of a 4-month-old to provide the infant with
    a. push-pull type toys
    b. snap beads and strings
    c. nesting blocks and cups
    d. soft squeeze toys with squeakers

12. A developmental assessment of a 9-month-old would be expected to reveal
    a. a two-to-three word vocabulary
    b. an ability to feed self with spoon
    c. the ability to sit steadily without support
    d. closure of both anterior and posterior fontanels

13. When evaluating growth and development of a 6-month-old infant, the nurse would expect the infant to be able to
    a. sit alone, display pincer grasp, wave bye-bye
    b. crawl, transfer toy from one hand to the other, display fear of strangers
    c. pull self to a standing position, release a toy by choice, play peek-a-boo
    d. turn completely over, sit momentarily without support, reach to be picked up

14. A 15-month-old infant is playing in the playpen. The nurse observing the infant's activities evaluates the infant's ability on physical tasks to be at the age-related norm when the infant is able to
    a. build a tower of six blocks
    b. walk across the playpen with ease
    c. throw all the toys out of the playpen
    d. stand in the playpen holding onto the sides

15. The nurse observes that an infant has head control, can roll over, but cannot sit up without support or transfer an object from one hand to another. Based on these facts, the nurse would conclude that the infant is developmentally at age
    a. 2 to 3 months
    b. 3 to 4 months
    c. 4 to 6 months
    d. 6 to 8 months

16. The nurse notes that a 22-month-old uses two- or three-word phrases (telegraphic speech), has a vocabulary of about 200 words, and frequently uses the word "me." The nurse would interpret the child's language development as being
    a. a severe lag
    b. slow for the child's age
    c. normal for the child's age
    d. advanced for the child's age

17. The social development of a 9-month-old is best promoted by having the infant
    a. manipulate soft clay
    b. pound on a peg board
    c. play peek-a-boo and bye-bye
    d. play with a large ball with a bell

18. The nurse should be aware that studies of children who have suffered prolonged maternal deprivation early in life indicate that these children
    a. are unable to love
    b. recall past experiences vividly
    c. are particularly conscious of time
    d. establish warm relationships with a mother substitute

19. A father brings in his 18-month-old son to the clinic. He asks the nurse why his son is so difficult to please, has temper tantrums, and annoys him by throwing food from the table. The nurse should explain that
    a. toddlers need to be disciplined at this stage to prevent the development of antisocial behaviors
    b. the child is learning to assert independence and his behavior is considered normal for his age
    c. this is the usual way that a toddler expresses his needs during the initiative stage of development
    d. it is best to leave the child alone in his crib after calmly telling him why his behavior is unacceptable

20. The nurse explains to the mother of a 2-year-old girl that the child's negativism is normal for her age and that it is helping her meet her need for
    a. trust
    b. attention
    c. discipline
    d. independence

21. The nurse teaches a mother that she can best help her toddler learn to control his or her own behavior by
    a. rewarding good behavior
    b. setting limits and being consistent
    c. punishing the child for misbehavior
    d. allowing the child to learn by mistakes

22. A two-year-old requires close supervision to protect against potential accidents because at this age the child's learning occurs primarily from
    a. playmates
    b. the parents
    c. older siblings
    d. trial and error

23. Play during infancy is
    a. initiated by the child
    b. a way of teaching how to share
    c. more important than in later years
    d. mostly used for physical development

24. When observing a toddler playing with other children in the playroom, The nurse would expect the toddler to engage in
    a. parallel play
    b. solitary play
    c. competitive play
    d. tumbling-type play

25. When teaching a mother how to prevent accidents while caring for her 6-month-old, the nurse should emphasize that this age child can usually
   a. sit up
   b. roll over
   c. crawl lengthy distances
   d. stand while holding onto furniture

26. Learning processes associated with a particular stage of development often are referred to as developmental tasks. A characteristic of developmental tasks is that
   a. tasks occur with predictable rhythm
   b. there is no uniform time for learning a task
   c. tasks are learned at the same age in children
   d. most developmental tasks are learned by school

27. An 11-year-old is diagnosed with acute lymphocytic leukemia (ALL) and the physician discusses the diagnosis and treatment with the family. The assessment data that indicate age-appropriate behavior for an 11-year-old regarding a diagnosis implying death and dying is that the child
   a. is rude, impolite, and insolent
   b. says that an uncle died and went to heaven
   c. is afraid to go to sleep for fear of not awakening
   d. tells the nurse that death is punishment for not being good

28. The nurse observes that a 4-year-old is having difficulty relating with the other children in the playroom. The nurse understands that it is normal for this age child to
   a. engage in parallel or solitary play
   b. be almost totally dependent on parents
   c. exaggerate and boast to impress others
   d. have fierce temper tantrums and negativism

29. A 2 1/2-year-old male child who has fallen from a tree tells his parents, "Bad, bad tree." The nurse recognizes that the child is within the cognitive developmental norm of Piaget's
   a. concrete operations
   b. concept of reversibility
   c. preconceptual operations
   d. sensorimotor development

30. The nurse is aware that a preschool child views death
   a. as permanent and irreversible
   b. in a frightening and horrible way
   c. as a departure from which the person returns
   d. without comprehending its meaning in any way

31. The average 5-year-old is incapable of
   a. tying shoelaces
   b. abstract thought
   c. making decisions
   d. hand-eye coordination

32. The nurse is aware that the toy that would be most appropriate for a 4-year-old would be a
   a. fuzzy stuffed animal
   b. six piece jigsaw puzzle
   c. lunch box filled with plastic figures
   d. blunt scissor and pictures to cut out

33. The nurse knows that an appropriate toy for a 6-year-old in a spica cast would be a
   a. ball and jacks
   b. game of checkers
   c. set of building blocks
   d. coloring book and crayons

34. The play activity that would be appropriate for a 6-year-old whose energy level has improved following an acute episode of Hirschsprung's disease would be
   a. using a set of building blocks
   b. finger painting on a large paper surface
   c. taking apart and putting together a truck
   d. drawing or writing with a pencil or marker

35. When assessing a 4-year-old the nurse would expect the child to
   a. ask the definitions of new words
   b. have a vocabulary of 1500 words
   c. name two or three different colors
   d. use just three- or four-word sentences

36. The nurse is aware that 5-year-olds engage in play that is known as
   a. parallel
   b. ritualistic
   c. aggressive
   d. cooperative

37. For a 10-year-old boy with rheumatoid arthritis in a two-bed room, the best roommate would be
   a. a 12-year-old girl with colitis
   b. a 9-year-old boy with asthma
   c. a 10-year-old girl with a fractured femur
   d. an 11-year-old boy with an appendectomy

38. When planning self-care that would foster independence, the nurse would expect a 4-year-old child to be able to
   a. button a shirt
   b. tie shoe laces
   c. part and comb hair
   d. cut the meat at dinner

39. A fifteen-year-old girl is grounded for 2 weeks by her parents for smoking in school. The adolescent tells the school nurse, "It's not fair that I get punished when my friends get away with doing the same thing." The nurse's most appropriate response would be
    a. "The others will pay someday for lying to school authorities."
    b. "I intend to report your friends to the principal so they can also be punished."
    c. "It is difficult enough to get teenagers to tell the truth. When parents don't act it reinforces deceptive behavior."
    d. "When errors in judgment are made, people must be prepared to take the consequences of their actions."

40. The mother of a 15-year-old female who is being treated for allergies privately tells the nurse that she thinks her daughter is becoming a hypochondriac. The nurse can be most therapeutic by
    a. discussing the underlying causes of hypochondriasis
    b. discussing the developmental behavior of adolescents
    c. explaining the potentially serious complications of allergies
    d. explaining that the mother may be transferring her own fears to her daughter

41. The nurse is aware that babies born to very young mothers are at risk for neglect or abuse because adolescents characteristically
    a. do not plan for their pregnancies
    b. cannot anticipate the baby's needs
    c. are involved in seeking their own identity
    d. resent having to give constant care to the baby

42. A day after an explanation of the effects of surgery to create an ileostomy, a 68-year-old male client remarks to the nurse, "It will be difficult for my wife to care for a helpless old man." These comments by the client regarding himself are an example of Erikson's conflict of
    a. initiative vs. guilt
    b. integrity vs. despair
    c. industry vs. inferiority
    d. generativity vs. stagnation

43. Nursing actions for the elderly should include health education and promotion of self-care. When dealing with the elderly the nurse should
    a. encourage exercise and naps
    b. strengthen the concept of ageism
    c. reinforce clients' strengths and promote reminiscing
    d. teach about a high carbohydrate diet and focus on the present

44. The nurse is preparing a health program for senior citizens in the community. The nurse teaches the group that physical findings that are normal in older people include
    a. a loss of skin elasticity and a decrease in libido
    b. impaired fat digestion and increased salivary secretions
    c. an increase in body warmth and some swallowing difficulties
    d. increased blood pressure and decreased hormone production in women

45. An 89-year-old client with osteoporosis is admitted to the hospital with a compression fracture of the spine. The nurse understands that a factor of special concern when caring for an elderly client is the client's
    a. inability to recall recent facts
    b. irritability in response to deprivation
    c. inability to maintain an optimal level of functioning
    d. gradual memory loss resulting from change in environment

46. Studies have shown that the grieving process may last longer for people who have
    a. feelings of guilt
    b. failed to remarry within three years
    c. ambivalent feelings about the death
    d. had a close relationship with their family

47. The occurrence of chronic illness is greatest in
    a. older adults
    b. adolescents
    c. young children
    d. middle-aged adults

48. When reaching the point of acceptance in the stages of dying, a client's behavior may reflect
    a. apathy
    b. euphoria
    c. detachment
    d. emotionalism

49. The nurse knows that Alzheimer's disease is characterized by
    a. transient ischemic attacks
    b. remissions and exacerbations
    c. rapid deterioration of mental functioning because of arteriosclerosis
    d. slowly progressive deficits in intellect, which may not be noted for a long time

50. The nurse should provide a confused client with an environment that is
    a. familiar
    b. variable
    c. challenging
    d. nonstimulating

Practice Test Two Answers and Rationale

1. c
   a. A high sperm count is optimum, but only one sperm is needed to penetrate the ovum.
   b. Conception takes place in a fallopian tube, not the uterus.
   c. Conception occurs when one sperm penetrates one ovum and creates a viable zygote.
   d. The sperm penetrates the ovum in a fallopian tube and then the impregnated ovum travels down the tube to the uterus.

2. b
   a. This is another name for the umbilical cord.
   b. The amnion encloses the embryo and the shock-protective amniotic fluid in which the embryo floats.
   c. The chorion is the outermost membrane; it does not secrete fluid.
   d. The yolk sac contains the stored nutrients of the ovum.

3. b
   a. Lightening is the descent of the fetus into the birth canal.
   b. The word originates from the Middle English word *quik*, which means alive.
   c. Ballottement is the bouncing of the fetus in the amniotic fluid against the examiner's hand.
   d. Engagement occurs when the presenting part is at the level of the ischial spines.

4. b
   a. The first trimester is the period of organogenesis, when cells differentiate into major organ systems.
   b. This is the period in which the fetus stores deposits of fat.
   c. Growth is occurring, but fat deposition does not occur during this period.
   d. This is the period of the blastocyst, when initial cell division takes place.

5. a
   a. Sucking meets oral needs, which are primary during infancy.
   b. An infant of a few days is probably too young to focus well on a mobile; in addition, the infant will be placed in a side-lying position postoperatively and thus would not be able to focus on the mobile.
   c. Two-day-old infants are not yet developmentally capable of enjoying a soft cuddly toy.
   d. This is not a developmental need.

6. c
   a. Most infants are on a demand feeding schedule, not a routine schedule; demand feeding provides for individuality.
   b. This is too limited; the parents need a broader discussion of infant behaviors.
   c. This information assists parents to understand the unique features of their newborn and promotes interaction and care during periods of wakefulness.
   d. Printed instructions are inadequate if unaccompanied by a discussion.

7. d
   a. This tests for the grasp reflex, not the Moro reflex.
   b. This tests for the Babinski reflex, not the Moro reflex.
   c. Although this tests the Moro reflex, it is not the best way; really tests the baby's hearing.
   d. Changes in equilibrium stimulate this neurologic reflex in an infant under the age of 6 months; the movements should be bilateral and symmetric; a loud noise causes the same reaction (startle reflex), but using noise as a stimulus really tests hearing.

8. a
   a. Head lag in an infant 6 months old is abnormal and is frequently a sign of cerebral damage.
   b. The ability to sit unsupported is achieved at 7 to 8 months.
   c. The Babinski reflex is normally present until 12 months of age.
   d. The tonic reflex and grasp reflex usually disappear at 2 and 3 months.

9. c
   a. A push-pull toy is appropriate for the older infant (9-12 months) and the toddler because it encourages walking.
   b. These are inappropriate; a child at this age puts toys in the mouth; playing with blocks requires motor development beyond this age.
   c. A stuffed animal is the most appropriate toy for the 6-month-old because it is safe and cuddly and requires only gross motor movement.
   d. Shape-matching toys require intellectual and motor development beyond that of this age-group.

10. d
   a. A 1-year-old child is too young for a book.
   b. The potential for injury is too great for a 1-year-old on a rocking horse.
   c. A stuffed animal would not be kept in a playroom because it could not be washed between use by different children.
   d. A plastic toy that squeaks provides auditory, tactile, and visual stimulation.

11. d
   a. This is appropriate for a child 12 to 24 months of age.
   b. This is appropriate for a child 10 to 12 months of age.
   c. This is appropriate for a child 16 months of age.
   d. This is appropriate for a 4-month-old, the child enjoys squeezing and hearing the sound of the squeaker.

12. c
   a. A two- to three-word vocabulary is an expectation of a 12-month-old child.
   b. This is accomplished by the 2-year-old, not the 9-month-old.
   c. This usually occurs by 8 months.
   d. Whereas the posterior fontanel is closed by age 2 months, the anterior fontanel closes between ages 12 to 18 months.

13. d
   a. These abilities should be developed by 10 months of age.
   b. Same as answer a.
   c. Same as answer a.
   d. These abilities are age appropriate for the 6-month-old.

14. b
   a. This is not usually true until the child is 2 years old.
   b. At 15 months, strength and balance have improved, and an infant can stand and walk alone.
   c. Infants are very capable of throwing toys.
   d. Children 9 to 12 months of age can stand with support.

15. c
   a. The ability to roll over is achieved by approximately 5 months of age.
   b. Same as answer a.
   c. Head control and rolling over are achieved at 4 and 5 months, respectively. Transferring objects from one hand to another and sitting unsupported are achieved at 7 and 8 months.
   d. Transferring objects from hand to hand is usually achieved in approximately 7 months.

16. c
   a. A child with a severe developmental lag would have no obvious recognizable speech pattern and would only make a few sounds.
   b. A child slow for this age would have a smaller vocabulary and would use only single words to identify familiar objects.
   c. Brief messages, with only essential words included (telegraphic speech), are a normal pattern for a child 18 months to 2 1/2 years of age.
   d. A child advanced for this age would have a larger vocabulary and would use 3- to 4- word sentences rather than telegraphic speech.

17. c
   a. This is age-appropriate play for the toddler; it promotes gross and fine motor development, not social development.
   b. This is age-appropriate play for preschoolers; it helps develop motor, not social, skills.
   c. These age-appropriate games help the infant's social development by fostering a sense of object constancy and object permanence.
   d. This is age-appropriate play for an older child; it promotes psychomotor, not social, development.

18. a
   a. A child learns to love others by the love received. When love is received, the child feels worthy of being loved and can share this feeling with others.
   b. Studies do not address this issue.
   c. Same as answer b.
   d. These children have difficulties forming attachments to people.

19. b
- a. This is untrue; excessive discipline leads to feelings of shame and self-doubt, the major crisis at this stage of development.
- b. The psychosocial need during the early toddler age is the development of autonomy. The toddler objects strongly to discipline.
- c. The sense of initiative is attained during the preschool age, not during the toddler age.
- d. It is frightening for a child to be left alone; it leaves the child with feelings of rejection, isolation, and insecurity.

20. d
- a. This is the developmental task achieved in infancy.
- b. Although this is a factor, toddlers assert themselves in an attempt to attain more autonomy.
- c. Children do not assert themselves to obtain discipline.
- d. The toddler is in Erikson's stage of acquiring a sense of autonomy. The negativism is the result of the child's need to express her will and test out her environment.

21. b
- a. Rewards should not always be necessary for good behavior; they will become expected.
- b. Children learn socially acceptable behavior when consistent, reasonable limits that provide guidelines are established.
- c. Authorities vary on their attitudes about punishment; punishment should not become the major means of teaching children to control their behavior.
- d. This is not always safe or reasonable for very young children.

22. d
- a. The toddler is still learning from own experiences not from others; this is the level of parallel, not interactive, play.
- b. The toddler is still attempting to distinguish self as separate from the parents; the struggle for autonomy limits learning from parents.
- c. The struggle for autonomy at this age limits learning from older siblings, even though the toddler attempts to copy their behaviors; older siblings often are not good role models because they tend to be careless.
- d. The child is developing autonomy, is curious, and learns from own experience.

23. d
- a. Play during infancy is usually initiated by the parent.
- b. Children do not begin to share until the preschool years.
- c. Play is important throughout childhood.
- d. Play during infancy (solitary) promotes physical development. For example, mobiles strengthen eye movement, large beads promote fine finger movement, and soft toys encourage tactile sense.

24. a
- a. The toddler is still dependent on the mother, is narcissistic, and still plays alone, but is aware of others playing nearby.
- b. Solitary play or onlookers' play is characteristic of the 1- to 2-year-old.
- c. Competitive play would be seen in school-age children.
- d. Tumbling-type play is not a commonly accepted term used to refer to how play incorporates other children.

25. b
- a. Sitting up unsupported is accomplished by most children at 7 to 8 months of age.
- b. Muscular coordination and perception are developed enough at 6 months so the infant can roll over. If unaware of this ability of the infant, the mother could leave the child unattended for a moment to reach for something and the chid could roll off the crib.
- c. Crawling takes place at about 9 months of age.
- d. Standing by holding onto furniture is accomplished by most children between 8 and 10 months.

26. b
- a. Tasks are more often learned in spurts than in a uniform, predictable rhythm.
- b. Although there is a time range, there is no specific time for a developmental task.
- c. Children differ in the ages at which they learn tasks.
- d. The entire life cycle requires the learning of developmental tasks.

27. a
   a. This is appropriate for an 11-year-old who sees dying as loss of control over every aspect of living; the child may convey this meaning by physically attempting to run away or by pushing others away by rude behavior; it is a plea for some self-control and power.
   b. This is characteristic of the toddler who is egocentric and has a vague separation of fact and fantasy, which makes it impossible to understand the absence of life.
   c. This is characteristic of the preschooler who does not have logical thinking.
   d. This is more typical of the adolescent who sees deviation from accepted behavior as the reason for becoming ill.

28. c
   a. Four-year-olds engage in more advanced cooperative play.
   b. This is highly unusual for 4-year-olds as they are striving toward more initiative and less dependence.
   c. Four-year-olds boast, exaggerate, and are impatient, noisy, and selfish.
   d. The tendency toward tantrums and negativism should have waned by 4 years of age.

29. c
   a. This is related to school-age children.
   b. This is a phase of concrete operations seen in school-age children.
   c. In the toddler, two- and three-word phrases are used with an increased vocabulary; attributing lifelike qualities to inanimate objects is also associated with preconceptual thought.
   d. This is related to infants.

30. c
   a. This is the concept of death held by children 9 or 10 years of age; death is viewed as reversible by the preschooler.
   b. The early school-age child of 6 or 7 years personifies death and sees it as horrible and frightening; this is consistent with the concrete thinking present at this age.
   c. Between the ages of 3 and 5 years, death is viewed as a departure or sleep, which is reversible.
   d. Children of all ages have some concept of death.

31. b
   a. A 5 year-old is capable of tying laces.
   b. Piaget stresses that age 7 is the turning point in mental development. New forms of organization appear at this age that mark the beginning of logic, symbolism, and abstract thought.
   c. A toddler is capable of making simple decisions.
   d. An infant is capable of hand-eye coordination.

32. c
   a. This is more appropriate for an infant.
   b. This is below the child's developmental level.
   c. A child this age loves to collect and manipulate; this meets the need to develop fine motor skills.
   d. The child is too young for scissors and fragile toys.

33. d
   a. The child will not have enough mobility to engage in this type of play and is too young for this activity.
   b. The child is too young for this activity; children of 7 or older are able to play checkers.
   c. Because of the spica cast, the child will not have enough mobility to play with this type of toy.
   d. This is appropriate for the child's age and suited to the child's limited motion.

34. d
   a. This would be appropriate for preschoolers whose imaginations are unlimited.
   b. This would be appropriate for preschoolers who enjoy experimenting with different textures.
   c. This would be appropriate for preschoolers who like repetition.
   d. This provides a 6-year-old, who is of school age, an appropriate way to express feelings, either by writing or drawing pictures.

35. b
   a. At 5 years of age, children ask the definitions of new words.
   b. Because of expanded experiences and developing cognitive ability the 4-year-old should have a vocabulary of approximately 1500 words.
   c. At 2 1/2 to 3 years of age, children can name colors.
   d. At 3 years of age, children use 3- or 4-word sentences.

36. d
   a. This type of play is characteristic of 2-year-olds.
   b. This is a type of behavior, not a type of play.
   c. Same as answer b.
   d. This type of play is characteristic of 5-year-olds.

37. d
   a. Same-sex roommates are desirable for companionship and to maintain boy/girl separateness of this age group.
   b. Asthmatic children may have severe respiratory difficulties; this may be too stressful for the client who needs rest.
   c. Same-sex roommates are desirable for companionship and to maintain privacy needs.
   d. Ten-year-old boys prefer the company of the same sex and age group. Also, the client needs to avoid stressful situations that would tend to increase exacerbations.

38. a
   a. A 4-year-old can manage large buttons on a shirt.
   b. A child of 4 years can put on shoes but is usually unable to tie them until age 5.
   c. A child of 4 years will be able to comb but not part the hair.
   d. A child of 4 can handle a fork and spoon but cannot hold the meat with the fork to cut it with the knife; the child is usually 7 years old before this can be managed.

39. d
   a. This is false reassurance; there is no way to predict what will be the outcome of her friends' behavior in the future.
   b. The focus should be on pointing out that the girl should be accountable for her own behavior, not that her friends should also be punished.
   c. The focus should be on the girl's actions and not those of her friends' parents.
   d. As part of the maturation process, adolescents need to be made to accept the consequences of their actions.

40. b
   a. This does not educate the mother about concepts concerning the developing adolescent; a discussion about hypochondriasis may reinforce mother's concern.
   b. Adolescents are very aware of their changing bodies and become especially concerned with any alteration due to illness or injury.
   c. This does not address concepts related to growth and development of the adolescent and could cause unnecessary concern about the daughter's physical condition.
   d. This could reinforce the mother's concern as well as promote feelings of guilt; it does not include concepts about growth and development of the adolescent.

41. c
   a. Although this may be true, it is not the reason the baby is at risk for neglect or abuse.
   b. Same as answer a.
   c. Adolescent parents are still involved in the developmental stage of resolving their own self-identity; they have not sequentially matured to intimacy and generativity.
   d. Same as answer a.

42. b
   a. These are conflicts manifested in early childhood between 3 and 6 years.
   b. According to Erikson, poor self-concept and feelings of despair are conflicts manifested in the 65-and-older age group.
   c. These are conflicts manifested during the ages from 6 to 11 years.
   d. These are conflicts manifested during middle adulthood, 45 to 65 years.

43. c
   a. Exercise should be encouraged, but naps tend to interfere with adequate sleep at night.
   b. Reinforcing ageism would enhance devaluation of the older adult.
   c. Reinforcing strengths promotes self esteem; reminiscing is a therapeutic tool which provides a life review that assists adaptation and helps achieve the task of integrity associated with the elderly.
   d. A well balanced diet that also includes protein and fiber should be encouraged; the elderly need to put the past in perspective and a positive self-assessment should be supported.

44. d
   a. There are no changes in libido with aging; there is a loss of skin elasticity.
   b. Salivary secretions decrease, not increase, causing more difficulty with swallowing; there is some impairment of fat digestion.
   c. There is a decease in subcutaneous fat, decreasing body warmth; some swallowing difficulties occur because of decreased secretions.
   d. With aging, there is a significant increase in the systolic blood pressure and a slight increase in the diastolic blood pressure; hormone production is decreased with menopause.

45. c
    a. This can result from the aging process and the change in environment; it is not as important as the loss of function.
    b. This would be an expected response.
    c. The onset of disabling illness will divert an aged person's energies, making it difficult to maintain an optimum level of functioning.
    d. A gradual memory loss and some confusion can be expected; a sudden memory loss would be cause for alarm.

46. a
    a. Guilt feelings can prolong the grieving process because the individual is overwhelmed by both the guilt and grief, and consequently the energy needed to cope with both is excessive.
    b. There are no research data to support this.
    c. Ambivalent feelings about the deceased, not the death itself, can prolong grief.
    d. Usually the opposite is true; the support provided would hasten resolution of grief.

47. a
    a. As a result of the normal stresses on the body, the incidence of chronic illness increases in the elderly population.
    b. Younger individuals have greater physiologic reserves and chronic illnesses are not common.
    c. Same as answer b.
    d. Same as answer b.

48. c
    a. Although detached, the client is still concerned and may use this time constructively.
    b. Although resigned to death, the individual is not euphoric.
    c. When an individual reaches the point of being able intellectually and psychologically to accept death, anxiety is reduced and the individual becomes detached from the environment.
    d. At the stage of acceptance, the client is no longer angry or depressed.

49. d
    a. TIAs may precede a cerebral vascular accident; this is unrelated to Alzheimer's disease.
    b. Alzheimer's is a progressive, deteriorating disease.
    c. Alzheimer's is a slow, chronic deterioration of the brain; the role of arteriosclerosis is unclear.
    d. Alzheimer's disease is an insidious atrophy of the brain resulting in a gradually diminished intellect.

50. a
    a. Sameness provides security and safety and reduces stress for the client.
    b. Clients with this disorder do not do well in a constantly changing environment.
    c. A challenging environment would increase anxiety and frustration.
    d. A nonstimulating environment would add to the client's diminishing intellect.

APPENDIX: ERIKSON'S, FREUD'S, AND PIAGET'S STAGES OF DEVELOPMENT

Developmental Period	Erikson's Stages
Infancy (0 to 1 year)	Trust versus mistrust
Toddlerhood (1 to 2 years)	Autonomy versus shame and doubt
Early childhood (3 to 5 years)	Initiative versus guilt
Middle and late childhood (6 years to puberty)	Industry versus inferiority
Adolescence (puberty to 20 years)	Identity versus identity confusion
Early adulthood (20s, 30s)	Intimacy versus isolation
Middle adulthood (40s, 50s)	Generativity versus stagnation
Late adulthood (60s+)	Integrity versus despair

Ages	Freud's Stages
0 to 18 months	Oral
1 1/2 to 3 years	Anal
3 to 6 years	Phallic
6 years to puberty	Latency
Puberty through adulthood	Genital

Ages	Piaget's Stages
0 to 2 years	Sensorimotor stage
2 to 7 years	Preoperational stage
7 to 11 years	Concrete operational stage
11 to 15 years through adulthood	Formal operational stage

REFERENCES

Averill, J.R. (1968). Grief: Its nature and significance. *Psychological Bulletin, 6,* 721-748.

Baltes, P.B. (1987). Theoretical propositions of life-span developmental psychology: On the dynamics between growth and decline. *Developmental Psychology, 23,* 611-626.

Baltes, P.B., & Baltes, M.M. (1990). Psychological perspectives on successful aging: The model of selective optimization with compensation. In P.B. Baltes & M.M. Baltes (Ed.), *Successful aging: Perspectives from the behavioral sciences.* New York: Cambridge University Press.

Baumrind, D. (1971). Current patterns of parental authority. *Developmental Psychology Monographs, 1(Pt.2).*

Bedmar, R.L., Wells, M.G., & Peterson, S.R. (1989). *Self-esteem.* Washington, DC: American Psychological Association.

Brook, J.S., Brook, D.W., Gordon, A.S., Whiteman, M., & Cohen, P. (1990). The psychological etiology of adolescent drug use: A family interactional approach. *Genetic, Social, and General Psychology Monographs, 116,* 110-267.

Brown, R. (1973). *A first language: The early stages.* Cambridge, MA: Harvard University Press.

Buss, A.H., & Plomin, R. (1984). *A temperament theory of personality development.* New York: Wiley.

Chess, S., & Thomas, A. (1977). Temperamental individuality from childhood to adolescence. *Journal of Child Psychiatry,16,* 218-226.

Cumming, E., & Henry, W. (1961). *Growing old.* New York: Basic Books.

Dryfoos, J.G. (1990). *Adolescents at risk: Prevalence and prevention.* New York: Oxford University Press.

Dryfoos, J.G. (1993). Schools as places for health,mental health,and special services. In R. Takanishi (Ed.), *Adolescence in the 1990s.* New York: Teachers College Press.

Elkind, D. (1978). Understanding the young adolescent. *Adolescence, 13,* 127-134.

Erikson, E.H. (1968). *Identity: Youth and crisis.* New York: W.W. Norton.

Freud, S. (1917). *A general introduction to psychoanalysis.* New York: Washington Square Press.

Gilligan, C. (1982). *In a different voice.* Cambridge, MA: Harvard University Press.

Gould, R.L. (1978). *Transformations: Growth and change in adult life.* New York: Simon & Schuster.

Harter, S. (1990). Self and identity development. In S.S. Feldman & G.R. Elliott (Eds.), *At the threshold: The developing adolescent.* Cambridge, MA: Harvard University Press.

Izard, C.E. (1982). *Measuring emotions in infants and young children.* New York: Cambridge University Press.

Kohlberg, L. (1976). Moral stages and moralization: The cognitive-developmental approach. In T. Lickona (Ed.) *Moral development and behavior.* NY: Holt, Rinehart, & Winston.

Kuypers, J.A., & Bengston, V.L. (1973). Social breakdown and competence. A model of normal aging. *Human Development, 16,* 181-201.

Kübler-Ross, E. (1974). *Questions and answers on death and dying.* New York: Macmillan.

Levinson, D.J. (1978). *The seasons of a man's life.* New York: Knopf.

Maccoby, E.E., & Martin, J.A. (1983). Socialization in the context of the family: Parent-child interaction. In P.H. Mussen (Ed.), *Handbook of Child Psychology,* (4th ed., vol. 4). New York: Wiley.

National Association for the Education of Young Children (1986). *How to choose a good early childhood program.* Washington, DC: NAEYC.

Parten, M. (1932). Social play among preschool children. *Journal of Abnormal and Social Psychology, 27,* 243-269.

Piaget, J. (1932). *The moral judgment of the child.* New York: W.W. Norton.

Piaget, J. (1952). *The origins of intelligence in children.* New York: International.

Peck, R.C. (1968). Psychological developments in the second half of life. In B.L. Neugarten (Ed.), *Middle age and aging.* Chicago: University of Chicago Press.

Santrock, J.W. (1995). *Life-span development* (5th ed.). Madison, WI: Brown & Benchmark.

Saxton, D.F., Nugent, P.M., & Pelikan, P.K. (Eds.) (1996). *Mosby's comprehensive review of nursing,* (15th ed.). St Louis, MO: Mosby.

Saxton, D.F., Pelikan, P.K., Nugent, P.M., & Needleman, S.K. (Eds.) *Mosby's review questions for NCLEX-RN* (2nd ed.). St. Louis, MO: Mosby.

Schaie, K.W. (1977). Toward a stage theory of adult cognitive development. *Aging and Human Development, 8,* 129-138.

Schorr, L. (1989, April). *Within our reach: Breaking the cycle of disadvantage.* Paper presented at the biennial meeting of the Society for Research in Child Development, Kansas City.

Super, D.E. (1976). *Career education and the meanings of work.* Washington, DC: U.S. Office of Education.

INDEX